IN DUE SEASON

I0624317

*Essays on Novels of Development
by Caribbean Women Writers*

Lucy Wilson

University Press of America,® Inc.
Lanham · Boulder · New York · Toronto · Plymouth, UK

Copyright © 2008 by
University Press of America®, Inc.
4501 Forbes Boulevard
Suite 200
Lanham, Maryland 20706
UPA Acquisitions Department (301) 459-3366

Estover Road
Plymouth PL6 7PY
United Kingdom

Library of Congress Control Number: 2008926469
ISBN-13: 978-0-7618-4112-8 (paperback : alk. paper)
ISBN-10: 0-7618-4112-1 (paperback : alk. paper)

DEDICATION

To the memory of
O. R. Dathorne
(1934-2007)

Contents

Acknowledgments

I am grateful to Father Mike Engh, S.J., Dean of the Bellarmine College of Liberal Arts of Loyola Marymount University, and the College Scholarship/Research Committee for generous support during the completion of this book. Thanks also to Dave Killoran, Chair of the Loyola Marymount University English Department, for his unwavering enthusiasm and encouragement from beginning to end of this project. I am especially grateful to my past and present research assistants, Teah Goldberg and Jason Jenkins, for their invaluable help with all stages of this project. Thanks also to friends and family members who read portions of the book and offered helpful suggestions: Thomas F. Wilson, Sharon Locy, and Rebecca Cantor. I wish to thank Alan Wilde, friend and mentor since my graduate school days at Temple University, for decades of encouragement and sound advice. I am grateful as well to my medical doctors—James P. Sutton, Qineng Tan, and Irving Sobel— for keeping me functioning despite my eight-year struggle with Parkinson's disease. But my greatest debt of gratitude goes to my husband, Alan Cherry, without whose love, support, and computer savvy this book would not exist.

"Dialogic Interplay in Coming-of-Age Novels by West Indian Women Writers." First published in *Children's Literature Association Quarterly* 18.4 (1993-94): 177-182. By permission of Johns Hopkins University Press.

"The Novel of Relational Autonomy: West Indian Women Writers and the Evolution of a Genre." First published in *Orality, Literacy and the Fictive Imagination: African and Diasporan Literatures*. Ed. Tom Spencer-Walters. Troy, MI: Bedford Publishers Inc., 1998. 281-305. By permission of Tom Spencer-Walters and Bedford Publishers, Inc.

"Aging and Ageism in Paule Marshall's *Praisesong for the Widow* and Beryl Gilroy's *Frangipani House*." First published in *Journal of Caribbean Studies* 7.2/3 (1989/1990): 189-199. By permission of O. R. Dathorne.

"Reading Kincaid's *The Autobiography of My Mother*" First published in *Journal of Caribbean Studies* 13:3 (1998/1999): 181-190. By permission of O. R. Dathorne.

"'Women must have spunks': Jean Rhys's West Indian Outcasts." First published in *Modern Fiction Studies* 32.3 (1986): 439-448. Rpt. in *Critical Perspectives on Jean Rhys*. Ed. Pierrette Frickey. Washington, D.C.: Three Continents Press, 1990. 67-74. By permission of Johns Hopkins University Press.

"European or Caribbean: Jean Rhys and the Language of Exile." First published in *Frontiers: A Journal of Women Studies* 10.3 (1989): 68-72. Rpt. in *Literature and Exile*. Ed. David Bevan. Amsterdam and Atlanta: Rodopi, 1990. 77-89. Copyright c. 1989 by Frontiers Editorial Collective.

"Helen of the Culture Wars: Jean Rhys and the Critics." First published in *Wasafiri* 21.2 (2006):88-91. By permission of *Wasafiri*.

Foreword

The first academic conference I ever attended as a graduate student was held on a small island off the coast of Texas favored by thousands of college students who migrate there for spring break. I had written what I thought was a brilliant paper, and after cutting it from its original twenty-two pages to a tidy conference length, I was ready. Or so I thought. There was a nervous twitch in my stomach that was threatening to escalate into a full blown panic attack. Who was I trying to fool? I had no business being at a Caribbean literature conference, attempting to pass myself off as an academic with something to contribute. I picked up the phone and called the one person I knew who could give me advice and calm me down. I called Lucy Wilson, my former professor and mentor. She told me stories about her own conference experiences. She assured me that almost everyone gets nerves but that the key is not to allow the anxiety to defeat you, to struggle against and through it. The first conference is a rite of passage, the inaugural step toward an academic identity, a coming out party, a discovery of self. Then I understood: as a young woman gaining confidence in her voice, in her abilities, and in her identity, I was in the same situation as the young female protagonists in so many novels written by West Indian women. As a woman trying to find her own way, I relate to the women imagined and brought to vivid life by Paule Marshall, Jamaica Kincaid, Jean Rhys, and Zee Edgell. In my own way I am Selina Boyce, Annie John, Antoinette Cosway, Beka Lamb, even Toycie. It was just a matter of finding the strength to stand on my own two feet and the confidence to raise my female voice in a male dominated field and world.

The essays in this collection, with the exception of the Introduction, appeared in journals and anthologies between 1986 and 2006. The essays in Part One discuss the need for a new model of female development, as the traditional *bildungsroman* is incompatible with the world experienced by contemporary female characters from developing nations. As a form, the *bildungsroman* is far too limited and cannot fully encompass the female voice which has historically been suppressed. As a result, West Indian women have reinvented the traditional male-centered form in order to portray the emerging female voice and consciousness. The maturational experiences of these protagonists are often mirrored in the coming-of-age process of their home countries; the emerging female voice echoes the newly forming collective voice of a people and a nation.

The characters inhabiting these works learn that development is an ongoing process, one that brings the women closer to their communities while simultaneously pulling them away. Novels of adolescence give way to novels of adulthood and old age. Eventually, these women all learn that to live life successfully is to live it on their own terms, to overcome that which oppresses them, and find the confidence and strength in themselves to make decisions that are right for them. With varying degrees of success each woman does learn, and those of us who read about them learn as well.

The essays in Part Two analyze the major works of Jean Rhys, including *Wide Sargasso Sea* and *Voyage in the Dark*. Unlike the protagonists in novels by Paule Marshall and Jamaica Kincaid, who strive for independence and an identity apart from their families and community, Rhys's women are tied to a pre-ordained fate. Both Antoinette Cosway and Anna Morgan are sacrificial victims, willing participants in the historical drama set in motion by their slave-owning ancestors. Through their destruction, these two women will finally atone for "the sins of the fathers" (*Voyage* 53). Only the complete annihilation of Antoinette, who takes her own life, and Anna, who suffers a near fatal abortion, will satisfy the collective memory.

For the female protagonists discussed in this book, the coming-of-age process does not merely involve breaking away from their families and nations. Rather it is achieved by recognizing that there is a world outside themselves, a world they are both "a part of" and "apart from." They must discern the ways in which their voices and newly forged identities can engage with the larger society.

In this book, Lucy Wilson addresses the need, expressed in many novels written by West Indian women, for both the authors and their female protagonists to immerse themselves in their communities and nations: to join the dialogue that has traditionally been reserved for men. However, the need for women to join the discourse crosses all geographical boundaries. Lucy Wilson takes the lessons she has learned from strong West Indian female characters, and the creative minds that bring them to life, and in turn encourages all women to find strength in themselves. In doing so, she honors those who have gone before her and supports all the women following in her footsteps, one conference at a time.

Teah Goldberg
Claremont Graduate University

Introduction:
In Due Season: Coming of Age in Caribbean Literature

The Evolution of a Genre

Since the nineteen-eighties, critics of Anglophone Caribbean literature have celebrated the presence of the female voice and perspective in what had been an almost exclusively male domain. Writers such as Erna Brodber, Michelle Cliff, Merle Collins, Zee Edgell, Merle Hodge, and Jamaica Kincaid–to name just a few–have established a womanist literary tradition by means of a multiplicity of narrative voices, a diversity of perspectives, a movement away from linearity and closure, the use of a wide range of discourses, and an emphasis on interpersonal relationships in the development of autonomous individuals. In a 1994 interview, Jamaica Kincaid told Moira Ferguson that "West-Indian writing until very recently was all men and then, for some reason, it is now mostly women" (Ferguson 164). The significance of Kincaid's comment can be appreciated if one considers that as recently as 1980, C. L. R. James made the following remark to Daryl Dance: "We haven't produced the women writers as yet. George Lamming tells me that he is waiting for the woman in the Caribbean to write a novel which will state the position of the Caribbean. Well, he is waiting for her. I am waiting for her too" (quoted in Nair 137).

Twelve years later, women writers had made their mark. Lamming told Supriya Nair in 1992 "that women had forced the [male] writers to change their discourse and [he] recommended *Out of the Kumbla* for readings of women writers in the Caribbean" (n.12, 157). Today, so much critical attention is focused on the younger women writers that there is some danger of viewing them as a phenomenon without literary precedents. This would be a mistake, however. The West Indian male writers who came of age during the first half of the twentieth century adapted the European *Bildungsroman* to reflect the reality of life in England's Caribbean colonies. Their contributions set the stage for the radical transformation of the genre that has been achieved by the women writers.[1]

In the essays that follow, I refer initially to these innovative narratives as *novels of dialogic interplay*, and later as *novels of relational autonomy*. These essays represent twenty years of thinking and writing about Caribbean women writers' contribution to the evolution of a genre. In their hands the *Bildungsroman* has expanded its focus to include the stages of a woman's life from adolescence to old age, implicitly recognizing that *Bildung* (learning, education, refinement) occurs throughout the life cycle.

These novels of relational autonomy by West Indian women writers did not evolve in a vacuum. Between the European novels of "education" (by Wieland, Goethe, Dickens, Butler,. Maugham, Lawrence, Joyce and others) and

the novels of relational autonomy by West Indian women writers, stands an important body of *Bildungsromane* by West Indian male writers, including C. L. R.
James, George Lamming, Samuel Selvon and Michael Anthony, whose reputations
were established before the present generation of women writers had finished grade
school. These mid-century male writers initiated a significant break with the European model of adolescent development by questioning the traditional *Bildungsroman*'s idealization of Romantic individualism and by emphasizing the communal
aspect of life in Trinidad and Barbados.[2]

Caribbean writers, therefore, shifted the focus of the *Bildungsroman* from the
individual to the community, as George Lamming explains in his 1983 Introduction
to *In the Castle of My Skin*. Acknowledging that his novel and those of other Caribbean writers have "caused some difficulty for the conventional critic of the novel,"
Lamming explains: "The book is crowded with names and people, and although
each character is accorded a most vivid presence and force of personality, we are
rarely concerned with the prolonged exploration of an individual consciousness. It
is the collective human substance of the Village itself which commands our attention. The Village, you might say, is the central character" (xxxvi). Lamming's
method interrogates certain assumptions inherent in the *Bildungsroman*, assumptions regarding the self's autonomy and the inviolable rights of the (male, European,
bourgeois) individual. The emphasis on community and communal life leads to an
innovative model of adolescent development in which the individual is defined to a
much greater extent *in relation* to the community.

Conventional critics continue to experience difficulty with *In the Castle of My
Skin*, as evidenced by Neil Ten Kortenaar's disparaging remarks in a 1991 essay. He
refers to the novel's "ungainly style" and "erratic narrative." Criticizing Lamming's
"disorienting lack of commitment to the characters and their unfolding stories,"
Kortenaar adds: "Characters go unnamed because their individual selves are of no
importance; they are just the head teacher or the shoemaker" (47). Responding to
Kortenaar's "Eurocentric analysis," Viney Kirpal explains that Lamming's novel and
those by other Third World writers are not structured according to Western notions
of formal logic and sequential plot development: "For taken as a novel, Lamming's
text has autonomy of space and time, but taken as oral narrative it erases causal and
spatial relationships. It seeks to grow in meaning through juxtaposition of episodes
and through accretion rather than through attainment of a climax (as in English fiction)" (106). Also emphasizing the importance of orality, Sandra Pouchet Paquet
remarks in the 1991 Forward to the novel: "The polyphonic design of *In the Castle
of My Skin* underscores the transformational nature of Lamming's novelization of
childhood and autobiography. The oral traditions of the village are given great authority in the narrative" (xxiii). Supriya Nair also notes the importance of oral traditions "in the dramatic and poetic dialogues that constantly break up the prose" and
undermine traditional narrative strategies (8).

The aspects of the novel that Kortenaar finds ungainly and erratic are in fact the
very qualities that elevate the prose to poetic heights. Take, for example, the first
time the narrative shifts from G.'s first-person point of view to the collective third-
person narrator:

Miss Foster. My mother. Bob's mother.
It seemed they were three pieces in a pattern which remained constant. The flow of
its history was undisturbed by any difference in the pieces, nor was its evenness
affected by any likeness. . . . Outside at the street corner where villagers poked
wreckage from the blocked canal, [the pattern] had absorbed another three, four,
fourteen. But there was no change in the increase. . . . In the broad savannah
where the grass lowcropped sang in the singeing heat the pattern had widened. Not
three, nor thirteen, but thirty. Perhaps three hundred. Men. Women. Children. The
men at cricket. The children at hide and seek. The women laying out their starched
clothes to dry. The sun let its light flow down on them as life let itself flow
through them. Three. Thirteen. Thirty. Three hundred. (25)

Ten pages later, when G. resumes his first-person narration, the pattern narrows: "In
the corner the sunlight had narrowed to a ray that struck down like a finger over the
three faces. Miss Foster, Bob's mother and my mother. Not thirteen, not thirty, but
three" (33).

Kortenaar contends that characters are nameless "because their individual
selves are unimportant," but when we as readers are allowed to "listen in" on a con-
versation between the shoemaker, the overseer's brother, Bob's father and Mr. Foster, it quickly becomes apparent that the unnamed shoemaker is an extremely important member of the community. He is the village philosopher who always reads the
newspapers and reads books whenever the opportunity presents itself. After reading
J. B. Priestly, the shoemaker "started to think of Little England as part of some gi-
gantic thing called colonial" (99). He is aware of civil unrest in Trinidad and reflects, prophetically, on the possibility of riots in Barbados. His interests range from
cricket to Marcus Garvey and Pan-Africanism, and for the dozen or so pages that he
holds court from behind the work bench in his little shop, his voice and opinions
displace the authority of both the first person and collective third person narrators.

In Chapter Ten, the narrative is wholly usurped by the incantatory ancestral
voice speaking through the sleeping village elder, Pa. For the duration of his dream,
Pa articulates a global vision that extends from Africa before the Middle Passage
through the voyages of Columbus and the creation of colonial slave states to the
present day: "A sailor called Christopher followed his mistake and those who come
later have added theirs" (210-11).

This is hardly a standard issue European-style *Bildungsroman*. G. is absent for
long periods in the novel, and when he reappears as narrator, his relationship with
the residents of Creighton Village, even with his boyhood friends, becomes increasingly strained. He attributes his alienation to his acceptance into the High School,
which is far more exclusive and competitive than the village school: "Those boys
who went from the village school to the High School had done so on the award of
the public examinations. There weren't many, and it wasn't easy for them to cope
with the two worlds. . . . Gradually the village receded from my consciousness although it wasn't possible for me to forget it" (218). In *The Colonial Legacy in Caribbean Literature*, Amon Saba Saakana describes the effects of colonial education:
"When slavery was abolished, under the persistent ravaging destruction of rebellion,
a new form of control was instituted: education." In the young colonial subject, this
education produced "a false consciousness, a jaundiced view of the world, which

put him at odds with the people he grew up with and who surrounded him" (102-3). Jamaica Kincaid recalls her own colonial education in a somewhat more positive light: "I had a very sort of abbreviated education. But I had a very good education . . . what I learned was memorizing Shakespeare and all this kind of nonsense. But I now know a lot of things about language that I can use against the people who educated me very well" (Ferguson 175).

The alienation of young Caribbean intellectuals from the communities that produced and nurtured them is a recurring motif in novels of adolescent development. Referring to the prototypical Caribbean *Bildungsroman*, C. L. R. James's *Minty Alley*, Kenneth Ramchand writes: "One of the novel's concerns is the mutually impoverishing alienation of the educated West Indian from the people . . . and it is one of the fundamental problems in West Indian social and political life today" (13). Ramchand's observation is reflected in many novels of development written since mid-century, including Lamming's *In the Castle of My Skin*, Hodge's *Crick Crack, Monkey*, Edgell's *Beka Lamb*, Kincaid's *Annie John*, and Cliff's *Abeng*. In all of these novels, class plays at least as important a role as race and gender in determining a character's experiential opportunities. Class conflict accounts as well for the importance of community and communal life in these novels. The protagonist's progress toward maturity is measured by his or her ability to connect with others across social, economic, and educational barriers. G.'s departure from Barbados at the end of *In the Castle of My Skin* is described in terms that suggest he is capitulating to historic and social forces, particularly the dismantling of Creighton Village as a result of Mr. Slime's treachery: "What could I do? What could any one of us do who knew the village, lived in it, loved it? What could any of us do about it? There was nothing I could do" (300).

When, at the end of *Annie John*, Kincaid's semi-autobiographical protagonist departs Antigua, her loneliness and isolation echo G.'s: "suddenly a wave of strong feeling came over me, and my heart swelled with a great gladness as the words 'I shall never see this again' spilled out inside me. But then, just as quickly, my heart shriveled up and the words 'I shall never see this again' stabbed at me. I don't know what stopped me from falling in a heap at my parents' feet" (145). Such self-imposed exile is a wrenching, traumatic experience that privileges autonomy at the expense of relationship. However, some West Indian coming-of-age novels end on a more positive note. At the end of *Beka Lamb*, Edgell's protagonist has achieved a degree of autonomy, but not at the expense of empathy and cooperation. Her relationships with her parents and grandmother are strengthened by her independence and sense of accomplishment. For Beka, coming of age entails a redefinition of herself in relation to her family, her best friend, and her community. Beka's dream of someday going into politics is one step closer at the end of the novel.

Similarly, Merle Collins's novel *Angel* ends with the protagonist's private wake for the restless spirits of her ancestors who were brought in shackles from Africa to labor on Delicia Estate. By taking an active role in the welfare of her country, by suffering and risking death to defend Grenada against the American invaders, Angel comes to terms with the colonial history of the Caribbean and achieves parity with her ancestors whose blood and tears saturate the land that the people hope, at long last, to call their own.

For George Lamming, "the collective human substance of the Village itself" is the central character of *In the Castle of My Skin*. The women writers have extended Lamming's political and aesthetic project. Their novels, like his, owe much to the oral art of storytelling. They have made relational autonomy not only a measure of maturity, but also the structuring principle of the novels themselves in which dialogue across generational, gender and political lines subverts the traditional perception of character as an individual and autonomous self. "Three. Thirteen. Thirty. Three hundred." Half a century ago, George Lamming subverted the traditional *Bildungsroman* in order to give voice to the community and to the ancestral spirit of Africa. Writers from the Anglophone Caribbean continue to depict a world struggling to break free of its colonial past while maintaining a vital link to that past by keeping the stories alive.

Illness as Metaphor

In the Caribbean novels written by male writers during the first half of the twentieth century, illness and injury frequently play an important role in the maturation of the protagonist. Perhaps due to the problematic relationship between girls and their bodies, in novels by women illness is often a rite of passage, a turning point in the protagonist's life, and the central structuring device of the narrative. Zee Edgell, Erna Brodber and Jamaica Kincaid associate illness with authenticity, freedom, and, for Edgell and Brodber, a reaffirmation of ancestral ties. A more coercive use of illness as metaphor occurs in the earlier works of two white creoles, Phyllis Shand Allfrey and Jean Rhys, who use these tropes to romanticize and mythologize the plight of the former ruling planter class. Illness may be physical or emotional, and madness plays a significant role in several novels.

For many African-Caribbean women writers, illness acts as a metaphor suggesting a rejection of externally imposed colonial values and a reaffirmation of indigenous and/or ancestral ties. In *Jane and Louisa Will Soon Come Home*, by Erna Brodber, the protagonist, Nellie Richmond, suffers a nervous breakdown. With the help and healing powers of her Rastafarian friend Baba, Nellie finds the strength to break out of the protective cocoon or "kumbla" that her family had woven around her consisting of middle-class pretensions, Eurocentric values, and pride in their white ancestry. With Baba's help, Nellie begins a spiritual journey that will enable her to reestablish contact with her African ancestry, the Creole language, and Afro-Jamaican folk culture. But first she must come to terms with her maturing woman's body and the dangerous power that accompanies menses: "'It' spoilt your life if you weren't careful! Yet 'it' gave you power, the power of a duppy that could send presents that nobody else could buy. . . . I was being given corrupting powers" (120-1).

In two of Jamaica Kincaid's novels, *Annie John* and *The Autobiography of My Mother*, illness also signifies rejection of externally imposed values and expectations, though in the case of Kincaid's protagonists, the transformation is more about personal freedom than reaffirmation of ancestral ties. When Western medicine fails to help Annie John, who is suffering a psychological and physical breakdown, her grandmother Ma Chess is called in to heal Annie by means of Obeah. Upon her recovery, Annie realizes that, more than anything else, she wants to leave her island, her mother, and the limitations imposed upon her by "this young lady business": the endless cycle of domestic drudgery that shuts women off from opportunities for achievement in the public domain. In *The Autobiography of My Mother,* a near fatal abortion leaves Xuela Richardson with a "broken womb," a metaphor loaded with patriarchal and misogynistic implications. But the novel contradicts this reading of Xuela's abortion and rejection of motherhood, instead equating childlessness with freedom and power. Xuela shares her knowledge of herbal "remedies" for pregnancy with other women, pleased that she can "extend such power to any other woman who asked for it" (115). Xuela's ability to deny life to the unborn has endowed her with godlike powers: "I would bear children, they would hang from me like fruit from a vine, but I would destroy them with the carelessness of a god" (97). In *The Autobiography of My Mother,* illness as unwanted pregnancy and abortion becomes a metaphor for female empowerment. Xuela decides to live completely on her own terms, to possess herself entirely, to be possessed by nothing and no one. By celebrating the liberating effects of childlessness and endowing abortion with sacramental qualities, Kincaid exposes the draconian choices that women are forced to make when societal expectations come into conflict with personal ambition and the desire for freedom. This conflict, which begins at puberty and extends throughout a woman's childbearing years, accounts for the recurring motif of psycho-sexual dysfunction in novels of female development: "What an abominable scrap heap thing is this thing womb" (*Jane and Louisa* 143).

Like Nellie Richmond, Annie John, and Xuela Richardson, Beka Lamb feels betrayed by gender when her best friend Toycie is expelled from school because she is pregnant. In Zee Edgell's novel *Beka Lamb*, Toycie goes mad and dies tragically, and Beka also experiences a breakdown, a prolonged period of mourning for her beloved friend. However, Beka recovers, finds the strength to go on, and discovers that she is stronger, more intelligent, and more creative than she had given herself credit for. Although Beka feels that she and her country have "bruk down," her friend and mentor Sister Gabriela tells her:

> You must go as far as the limitations of your life will allow. Find a way to do what you can, even though things seem to be crashing all around you. Sometimes they are not breaking down at all, sometimes things are taking a different shape. Try to recognize the pattern even if it is one you don' like, then maybe you can do something about it. (116)

Sister Gabriela's advice reflects the metaphoric role that illness plays in many late 20th century novels by Caribbean women writers. Physical and often mental collapse coincides with the breakdown of ties to home and family, as well as the transition from child to woman. This transitional time tests the protagonist's courage and strength, and more often than not she emerges phoenix-like from the ashes of her childhood to take her place in the life of her community, her country, or even beyond.

Unlike the generation of West Indian women writers of color (including Brodber and Kincaid) who achieved international recognition in the seventies and eighties, two white Creole writers from an earlier generation—Jean Rhys and Phyllis Shand Allfrey—use metaphors of illness to obfuscate rather than illuminate. In Allfrey's *The Orchid House*, three sisters return to Dominica from self-imposed exile, each with a plan to remedy the rapidly deteriorating situation at home. The situation is beyond hope, however, as is signified by the multitude of illness metaphors: their former nurse and faithful family retainer, Lally, refuses to have a tumor cut out; their beloved cousin has tuberculosis; and their father is dying as a result of decades of drug addiction. The family is paying the price for generations of greed and abuse. Like the parasitical bromeliad that towers above a young tree, "sapping it like a disease but growing to be even stronger and more beautiful than the tree itself" (Allfrey 178), the planter class exploited the people and resources of Dominica, but now they are no better than "white cockroaches," as Jean Rhys's former slave owners are called in *Wide Sargasso Sea*.

Allfrey has chosen the three illnesses that Sontag discusses in "Illness as Metaphor": cancer, tuberculosis, and [drug addiction induced] insanity. The narrator, Lally, makes the metaphor explicit: "Beauty and disease, beauty and sickness, beauty and horror: that was the island" (Allfrey 75). Lally's words are echoed by Antoinette Cosway in the opening pages of *Wide Sargasso Sea* when she describes the garden at Coulibri estate as a paradise lost with the end of slavery, where twice a year the snaky tentacles of the octopus orchid were completely hidden by beautiful flowers. The influence of Roman Catholicism on the child Ella Gwendolen Rees Williams, who later took the name Jean Rhys, has been noted by Elaine Savory (110) and may account for the thread of remorse and repentance that runs through *Wide Sargasso Sea* and the earlier novels. In *Voyage in the Dark*, Anna Morgan's family history haunts her in a recurring memory of a slave list she once saw at Constance Estate. Anna's English stepmother makes the connection explicit: "The sins of the fathers Hester said shall be visited upon the children unto the third and fourth generation" *(Voyage* 53).[3]

Metaphors of illness recast the historical drama, turning victors into victims and vice versa. In *Wide Sargasso Sea,* when Antoinette is injured by a rock thrown by Tia during the burning of Coulibri Estate, Antoinette momentarily exchanges places with her former friend: "We stared at each other, blood on my face, tears on hers. It was as if I saw myself. Like in a looking-glass" (45). Later in the novel, Antoinette's husband compares the beauty of the mulatta servant girl Amelie to a cancer: "A lovely little creature but sly, spiteful, malignant perhaps, like so much else in this place" (65). He implies that her beauty and that of the island have conspired to seduce him, rob him of volition, in essence enslave him. According to Susan Sontag: "For more than a century and a half, tuberculosis provided a metaphoric equivalent for delicacy, sensitivity, sadness, powerlessness; while whatever seemed ruthless, implacable, predatory, could be analogized to cancer. . . . Cancer was never viewed other than as a scourge; it was, metaphorically, the barbarian within" ("Illness" 61). Rochester's cancer analogy implicitly casts Amalie as a female Caliban, thus exonerating the English gentleman from any responsibility when he beds her and sends her away in the morning.

Sontag maintains that romanticizing of tuberculosis in the late eighteenth and early nineteenth centuries led directly to the "cult of thinness" in twentieth century women's fashions. Furthermore, mental illness has replaced TB as the disease of choice among the leisured classes: "Not TB but insanity is the current vehicle of our secular myth of self-transcendence. The romantic view is that illness exacerbates consciousness. Once that illness was TB; now it is insanity that is thought to bring consciousness to a state of paroxysmic enlightenment" ("Illness" 36). Sontag's conflation of insanity and self-transcendence is an apt description of Antoinette's mental state at the end of *Wide Sargasso Sea*. Consumed with hatred for the man who has taken her money and property but rejected her love, Antoinette withdraws behind a wall of silence. She leaves her husband hungry for, in his words, the "magic and the secret I would never know. . . . Above all I hated her. For she belonged to the magic and the loveliness. She had left me thirsty and all my life would be thirst and longing for what I had lost before I found it" (*WSS* 172). Observing that his wife "was silence itself" (168), Antoinette's husband consigns her to the ranks of the apparently mad women and men who are the keepers of the secret: "Very soon she'll join all the others who know the secret and will not tell it. . . . She's one of them" (172).

If Antoinette is mad, she is so in the manner that Michel Foucault describes as the pre-Renaissance association of madness with "the presence of imaginary transcendences" (*Madness* 58). This view of insanity does not cast Antoinette in the role of victim; rather, it undermines the notions of victim and victor by deconstructing binary thinking. Like tuberculosis in previous centuries, this view of madness affirms "the value of being more conscious, more complex psychologically. Health becomes banal, even vulgar" (Sontag, "Illness" 26).

Allfrey embodies this cavalier attitude of contempt for the mundane in the sisters' beloved cousin Andrew who is dying of "consumption." When Stella berates him for giving up his life "without a struggle," Andrew rationalizes that dying young is preferable to old and even middle age: "what is life, anyway, with bodies like that and half-blind eyes?" (55). Confronted with the decline of the planter class and the demise of the world of privilege and comfort into which he was born, Andrew adopts a stance reminiscent of the protagonist's in *Axel*, a play by French symbolist August Villiers de L'Isle-Adam. Axel is so certain that he and Sara have reached the apex of mortal existence that he announces disdainfully, before he and his beloved commit suicide, "Live? Our servants will do that for us" (183).

Jamaica Kincaid has commented on the nihilistic posturing of female characters in novels by white women, and she contrasts the "crumbling" protagonists of Duras and Rhys to black characters:

> Yes, in African writers and Caribbean writers, the women are very strong. Yes, and it is not phony. It is not borrowed. The strange thing is that the Americans, the women from the center of the world, lack that sense of self-invention or renewal, self-discovery. They don't have that, unless of course they are a repressed group like the black women in America. But the white women in America and European

women, you know, they don't have that at all. . . . They are sort of decaying, they
sort of enjoy writing about decay in some enjoyable way. (Ferguson 177)

Kincaid attributes this to the white woman's investment in the status quo: "Even as
they are oppressed within their group, they are still of the privileged. I think that
change for them would be very threatening to their status because when we rebel we
want the whole thing washed away, turned upside down. But they can't do that because they would lose something too" (Ferguson 177).

In novels by Afro-Caribbean writers, even elderly black women are strong.
Kincaid's Xuela Richardson is as proud and uncompromising at seventy as she was
in her prime. And the protagonists of Paule Marshall's *Praisesong for the Widow*
and Beryl Gilroy's *Frangipani House* have turned the infirmities and physical limitations of old age into opportunities for spiritual renewal.

Jean Rhys's novels do not fit the pattern; hence the placement of the three essays on Rhys in a section of their own. *Voyage in the Dark* is an anti-
Bildungsroman with Anna's coming of age corresponding to a decline in fortune,
failure in a profession, and a courtship plot run amok. Because *Wide Sargasso Sea*
is set in the first half of the nineteenth century, it has elements of the courtship plot,
but as a prequel to *Jane Eyre* written in the mid-twentieth century, the novel constitutes a critique of nineteenth-century attitudes toward women and a revisionist reading of Bronte's classic. While the weakness and decay that Kincaid perceives may
be due in part to the author's color and class, something else is at work here. Rhys
was born in 1890 and "discovered" in Paris by Ford Madox Ford at the height of the
modernist movement. Rhys's characters bear witness to the decline of European
civilization from the collapse of the plantation system with the end of slavery to the
First World War, the Great Depression, and World War II. Their typically modern
response to catastrophic historical events and acute personal hardship is to turn in-
ward, seeking refuge in militant solipsism and ironic detachment. The novels attempt to impose aesthetic order on the chaos of history by means of narrative inno-
vation: stream-of-consciousness, symbolism, and poetic language. "Modernist
literature is a literature of discontinuity, both historically, being based upon a sharp
rejection of the procedures and values of the immediate past, to which it adopts an
adversary stance; and aesthetically" (Drabble 658). Like Eliot in *The Waste Land*,
Rhys's characters "can connect / Nothing with nothing," but the novels themselves
are fragments of exquisite prose "shored against [the] ruins" of a crumbling world
(Eliot 46, 50).

Kincaid was born over half a century after Rhys, and her aesthetic is distinctly
postmodern: "Rejecting the possibility of totalizing orders, the adequacy of alternative worlds, the distance or detachment privileged by modernist writers together
with the (aesthetic) finality, resolution, and closure they aim to achieve, postmod-
ernism adopts, as Merleau-Ponty had, a perspective deliberately located within the
world" (Wilde 50-1). Contemporary Caribbean women writers create characters
who are actively shaping the postcolonial world around them. These writers have
responded to George Lamming's call for a woman novelist who would "state the
position of the Caribbean." That position can be summarized in two words: strong
women. The women in these novels turn the burden of history into a cherished re-

sponsibility to their courageous ancestors—the men and women who survived the Middle Passage and hundreds of years of bondage—and to future generations:

> Mother, one stone is wedged across the hole in our history
> and sealed with blood wax.
> In this hole is our side of the story. . . .
> It is the half that has never been told, some of us
> must tell it. (Goodison 138)

Notes

1. Coming-of-age novels by West Indian women writers represent the culmination of Bakhtin's vision of the novel as genre, for in them human consciousness achieves the dialogic awareness that existed in nascent form in the *Bildungsroman*. Bakhtin singles out the *Bildungsroman* for special praise because the protagonist's "individual emergence is inseparably linked to historical emergence. . . . He emerges *along with the world* and he reflects the historical emergence of the world itself. . . . It is as though the very foundations of the world are changing, and man must change along with them" (Bakhtin, "The *Bildungsroman*" 23-4). Through an "exquisite balancing act" between the desire for independence and the longing for intimacy, women writers from the Caribbean have contributed to the evolution of the novel genre by overcoming what Evelyn Fox Keller sees as a dichotomy between autonomy and relatedness (100). For further discussion, see "The Novel of Relational Autonomy" in this volume.

2. The *Bildungsroman* has a long history, extending back two centuries and representing a pivotal development in the evolution of the novel as genre. According to Jeffrey L. Sammons, the *Bildungsroman* is an "intensely bourgeois" phenomenon; "it carries with it many assumptions about the autonomy and relative integrity of the self," assumptions that have become increasingly difficult to sustain in the modern world (42). The historical and cultural roots of the male *Bildungsroman* and the female courtship novel in nineteenth-century bourgeois European society are philosophically incompatible with the depiction of characters whose existence is premised on hundreds of years of oppression and exploitation by those same European societies. For more on the relationship between the bourgeois genre and post-/neo-colonial realities, see Maria Helena Lima's "Decolonizing Genre" and Maria Karafilis's "Crossing the Borders of Genre."

3. In both of Rhys's Caribbean novels, *Voyage in the Dark* and *Wide Sargasso Sea*, primitivist tropes enable Rhys to reimagine the role of the white Creole in the Caribbean. These motifs abound in *Voyage*, from the stereotypical, "Being black is warm and gay" (31), to the historically significant, as when Anna Morgan recalls something she once read about the Carib Indians of Dominica: "The Caribs indigenous to this island were a warlike tribe and their resistance to white domination, though spasmodic, was fierce. . . . But they are now practically exterminated" (105). Rhys's conflicted feelings regarding her family's role in Caribbean history are mirrored in her attitude toward West Indians of color. Like her Welsh father, Jean Rhys

"was capable of holding both liberal and racist views" (Savory 6). Veronica Gregg argues that the white creole demonstrates, toward mulattos and blacks, "a sense of proprietorship that allows for the recruitment of 'race' as an accessory of power and a trope of otherness" (43). Sue Thomas notes both the celebratory (natural, unin-hibited) and the derogatory (threatening, promiscuous) primitivist tropes that Rhys uses in her depiction of black West Indians (101). In all her novels, these tropes serve as a kind of shorthand or code for resistance to bourgeois norms, misogyny, hypocrisy, and even the inevitability of death and decay.

Works Cited

Allfrey, Phyllis Shand. *The Orchid House*. 1953. Washington, DC: Three Conti-nents, 1985.

Bakhtin, Mikhail M. "The *Bildungsroman* and Its Significance in the History of Realism (Toward a Historical Typology of the Novel)." *Speech Genres and Other Late Essays*. University of Texas Press Slavic Series 8. Trans. Vern W. McGee. Ed. Caryl Emerson and Michael Holquist. 1986. Austin: University of Texas Press, 1992.

Brodber, Erna. *Jane and Louisa Will Soon Come Home*. London: New Beacon, 1980.

Collins, Merle. *Angel*. London: The Women's Press, 1987.

Drabble, Margaret, ed. *The Oxford Companion to English Literature*. 5th ed. New York: Oxford, 1985.

Edgell, Zee. *Beka Lamb*. 1982. London: Heinemann, 1986.

Eliot, T. S. "The Waste Land." *The Complete Poems and Plays*. New York: Har-court, Brace & World, 1971.

Ferguson, Moira. "A Lot of Memory: An Interview with Jamaica Kincaid." *The Kenyon Review* 16.1 (1994): 163-188.

Foucault, Michel. *Madness and Civilization: A History of Insanity in the Age of Reason*. Trans. Richard Howard. 1961. New York: Vintage, 1982.

Goodison, Lorna. "Mother the Great Stones Got to Move." *Selected Poems*. 1992. Ann Arbor: University of Michigan Press, 2002.

Gregg, Veronica Marie. *Jean Rhys's Historical Imagination: Reading and Writing the Creole*. Chapel Hill: University of North Carolina Press, 1995.

Karafilis, Maria. "Crossing the Borders of Genre: Revisions of the 'Bildungsroman' in Sandra Cisneros's 'The House on Mango Street' and Jamaica Kincaid's 'An-nie John." *JMMLA* 31.2 (1998): 63-78.

Keller, Evelyn Fox. *Reflections on Gender and Science*. New Haven: Yale Univer-sity Press, 1985.

Kincaid, Jamaica. *Annie John*. 1983. NY: New American Library. 1986.

———. *The Autobiography of My Mother*. New York: Farrar, Straus and Giroux, 1996.

Kirpal, Viney. "George Lamming's *In the Castle of My Skin*: A Modern West In-dian Novel." *ARIEL* 28.2 (1997): 103-14.

Kortenaar, Neil Ten. "George Lamming's *In the Castle of My Skin*: Finding Promise in the Land." *ARIEL* 22.2 (1991): 43-53.

Lima, Maria Helena. "Decolonizing Genre: Jamaica Kincaid and the Bildungsroman." *Genre* 26.4 (1994): 431-459.

Nair, Supriya. *Caliban's Curse: George Lamming and the Revisioning of History*. Ann Arbor: University of Michigan Press, 1996.

Paquet, Sandra Pouchet. Forward. Lamming, George. *In the Castle of My Skin*.

Ramchand, Kenneth. Introduction. *Minty Alley*. By C. L. R. James. Jackson, MS: University Press of Mississippi, 1997.

Rhys, Jean. *Voyage in the Dark*. 1934. New York: W. W. Norton, 1982.

———. *Wide Sargasso Sea*. 1966. New York: W. W. Norton, 1982.

Saakana, Amon Saba. *The Colonial Legacy in Caribbean Literature*. Trenton, NJ: Africa World Press, 1987.

Sammons, Jeffrey L. "The *Bildungsroman* for Nonspecialists: An Attempt at Clarification." *Reflection and Action: Essays on the Bildungsroman*. Ed. James Hardin. Columbia, SC: University of South Carolina Press, 1991.

Savory, Elane. *Jean Rhys*. Cambridge, UK: Cambridge University Press, 1998.

Sontag, Susan. *Illness as Metaphor* and *AIDS and Its Metaphors*. 1977. New York: Picador, 1990.

Thomas, Sue. *The Worlding of Jean Rhys*. Contributions to the Study of World Literature 96. Westport, Connecticut: Greenwood, 1999.

Villieurs de l'Isle-Adam, Philippe Auguste. *Axel*. Trans. June Guicharnaud. Englewood Cliffs, NJ: Prentice-Hall, 1970.

Wilde, Alan. *Middle Grounds: Studies in Contemporary American Fiction*. Philadelphia: University of Pennsylvania Press, 1987.

PART ONE: Stages of Female Development

Dialogic Interplay in Coming-of-Age Novels by West Indian Women Writers

Since the nineteen eighties, a number of coming-of-age novels with female protagonists have emerged in the English-speaking Caribbean countries. In a recent article, Renee Hausmann Shea points out that these novels by Caribbean women writers have much to offer teachers of literature and their students in the United States, for whom the realities of life in the late twentieth century have more in common with the lives of their Caribbean counterparts than they have with the world of Goethe's Wilhelm Meister or even Joyce's Stephen Dedalus. Shea explains:

> The conflicts and contradictions of class and color, the dual history of colonized people, the ironies inherent in an educational system that enshrines one culture at the expense of any other are contemporary Caribbean women writers' subjects—and these are difficult realities. But they are the realities of today's multi-racial and multi-cultural America, and these works explore them with sensitivity, wit, and brilliant command of language. (40)

Although, as Shea points out, "few of these novels and stories were written expressly for adolescents," their protagonists are "bright, rebellious, intractably clever, and always strong-willed" adolescents whose problems and experiences evoked a very positive response among Shea's female high-school and college-preparatory students (36).[1]

Before beginning my discussion of such works by Jamaica Kincaid, Erna Brodber, Zee Edgell and Paule Marshall, it is helpful to look at the theoretical framework of the genre itself. These West Indian writers have not only made important contributions to the literature of adolescence; they have reimagined the entire concept of development, challenging their readers to rethink the way that they view themselves and inhabit the world. Carolyn Heilbrun maintains that "lives do not serve as models; only stories do that. And it is a hard thing to make up stories to live by" (37). Women writers from the West Indies are creating stories to serve as models for young women's lives by questioning both the traditional male *Bildungsroman* or quest plot and the female marriage or court-ship plot.[2] Their alternative to these limited and limiting narrative models acknowledges essential differences between girls and boys, women and men, but at the same time this new model of female development demands equality of opportunity and freedom from gender-based oppression for the female protagonists.

In the introduction to *The Voyage In: Fictions of Female Development*, Elizabeth Abel argues that the *Bildungsroman* was limited to the development of male protagonists because assumptions about the self's autonomy and integrity did not reflect the maturation experience of women. Abel cites several feminist theorists—including Nancy Chodorow, Carol Gilligan, and Jean Baker Miller—to illuminate this problem:

> Historically, only the masculine experience of separation and autonomy has been awarded the stamp of maturity. . . . A distinctive female "I" implies a distinctive value system and unorthodox developmental goals, defined in terms of empathy rather than achievement and autonomy. . . . Female fictions of development reflect the tensions between the assumptions of a genre that embodies male norms and the values of its female protagonists. (10-11)

Abel's view is shared by Sibel Erol who describes a distinctively female alternative to the male linear model: "Totality is not analogous with the ending of a linear progression . . . the end of the forwardly linear, physical journey is a psychologically backward circular journey into the dawn of the preoedipal totality with the mother" (7-8).

Not all feminist critics are comfortable with a distinctive female model of development, for the adventure or quest model has a certain appeal for both genders, especially now that young women in many cultures are no longer limited exclusively to domestic duties, and education and travel opportunities are available to girls as well as boys. Given that women are no longer excluded from the public realm, should the European *Bildungsroman* be appropriated by women writers for their female protagonists? Or is there something unique to the female experience that is inadequately served by the *Bildungsroman*'s emphasis on autonomy and individualism?

Ann R. Morris and Margaret M. Dunn observe that Chodorow and Gilligan have stirred up controversy with their emphasis on a male "separation-paradigm" and a female "connection-paradigm" because their argument is seen by some as perpetuating and legitimizing "a view of women as essentially different from men" (236; n. 4). Susan Fraiman worries that "those theories of female developmental fiction that recuperate a wholly different plot of spiritual growth and domestic relationships" will continue to marginalize women by remaining "too obligingly within the given contours of 'women's culture,' neglecting the troubling appeal and predominance of the *Bildiungsroman* for female figures" (143-4). Fraiman is uncomfortable with the *Bildungsroman*'s idealization of Romantic individualism, and she suggests that female coming-of-age narratives by nineteenth century English writers should be read "less as a wholly alternative structure than as an ironization and interrogation of the old" (126-7).

Caroline Heilbrun calls for a quest plot for female adventurers, a plot that allows for female ambition and achievement in the public domain: "Women need to learn how publicly to declare their right to public power. . . . Power is the ability to take one's place in whatever discourse is essential to action and the right to have one's part matter" (18). Nevertheless, Heilbrun acknowledges the need for women to view themselves collectively:

> I suspect that female narratives will be found where women exchange stories, where they read and talk collectively of ambitions, and possibilities, and accomplishments. I do not believe that new stories will find their way into texts if they do not begin in oral exchanges among women in groups hearing and talking to one another. As long as women are isolated one from the other, not allowed to offer other women the most personal accounts of their lives, they will

not be part of any narrative of their own. . . . There will be narratives of female lives only when women no longer live their lives isolated in the houses and the stories of men. (46-47)

Although Heilbrun is discussing autobiographies and "real" lives, the stories that inform the lives of real women are often the novels that they read as young adults; thus her position is not a purely academic matter. Do we want our young women—our daughters, granddaughters, students—to model their lives on the *Bildungsroman*'s Romantic individualism or on the "connection-paradigm" of Chodorow and Gilligan? Or is this a false dichotomy?

If, as Fraiman maintains, nineteenth-century British women writers opened a space for interrogation and critique within the *Bildungsroman* genre, Caribbean women writers are taking that interrogation to a new level by retaining what they see of value in the quest or adventure plot. Their protagonists are often headstrong, ambitious young girls with unquenchable curiosity about the world around them. They are usually good students who view education as a way out of the cycle of drudgery and domestic slavery. If they do not actually set out on a journey, the thought of travel is never far from their minds. Unlike their nineteenth-century English counterparts, these girls are not usually being groomed for marriage. Although premarital sex is still not regarded with approbation by society, they are not bound by the rigid moral code that Victorian England imposed on middle-class girls.

There is a difference, though, between such novels as *Annie John, Jane and Louisa Will Soon Come Home, Beka Lamb, Brown Girl, Brownstones* and the traditional *Bildungsroman*. This difference is one of degree, and it can be explained in terms of what Mikhail Bakhtin refers to as "an *active dialogic approach to one's own self*, destroying that naïve wholeness of one's notions about the self that lies at the heart of the lyric, epic, and tragic image of man" (*Dostoevsky's Poetics* 120). The novel, for Bakhtin, "is the characteristic text of a particular stage in the history of consciousness not because it marks the self's discovery of itself, but because it manifests the self's discovery of the other" (Holquist 75). The *Bildungsroman* epitomized the novel as genre for Bakhtin because in it the protagonist "emerges *along with the world* and he reflects the historical emergence of the world itself" (Bakhtin, "The *Bildungsroman*" 23). However, the *Bildungsroman* was limited by its continuing dependence on Romantic notions of individualism and the self's autonomy.[3] The novels by Caribbean women writers are not. From birth, the female protagonists in these coming-of-age narratives are defined by their connections to others. The novels unfold as the protean "other" takes on a variety of shapes: mother, friend, lover, community. While the novels are not entirely lacking in chronological, linear development, there is an equally compelling force within the narratives that traces the expansion of the protagonist's consciousness as she recognizes and acknowledges the complexity and variety of the world, defining herself in relation to it. This recognition is an ongoing process, not an isolated moment; since society is not external to her, as she grows in self-awareness, her knowledge of the world expands. These female novels of development are thus the culmination of Bakhtin's vision of the novel as genre, for in them human consciousness achieves the dialogic awareness that existed in nascent form in the *Bildungsro-man.*

To avoid confusion with the earlier form of the genre and to emphasize the special achievement of these female coming-of-age narratives, a new term is needed for these fictions. Perhaps we could borrow a phrase from Mitzi Myers and call them novels of "dialogic interplay," a term that would have the added benefit of connecting these works to works by one of the literary foremothers of today's generation of Anglophone writers.[4]

In female coming-of-age narratives by West Indian authors, the earliest manifestation of dialogic interplay occurs between daughters and mothers in a unique emotional tug-of-war. In the mind of an adolescent girl, "a regressive longing" for an "original pre-oedipal state of merging" with the mother is in conflict with an equal and opposite need "to separate from the mother," a struggle that "is particularly wrenching for girls, for to separate is to deny the mother, which for girls is also to deny some part of the self" (Natov 2). In *Annie John,* by Jamaica Kincaid, the narrator describes her life before puberty as " a paradise" because of the tremendous love that she and her mother felt for each other. With the onset of menstruation, Annie begins to feel bitterness and hatred toward her mother and toward "life in general," but hatred takes up residence in her heart without evicting the previous tenant, and the result is an intensely ambiguous emotion.

Kincaid's *At the Bottom of the River* is, like *Annie John,* a coming-of-age narrative, but the story is presented in fragments of surrealistic prose. A passage from "My Mother" captures the essence of this mother/daughter conflict:

> I lay on her bosom, breathless, for a time uncountable, until one day, for a reason she has kept to herself, she shook me out and stood me under a tree and I started to breathe again. I cast a sharp glance at her and said to myself, "So." Instantly I grew my own bosoms, small mounds at first, leaving a small, soft place between them, where, if every necessary, I could rest my own head. Between my mother and me now were the tears I had cried, and I gathered up some stones and banked them in so they formed a small pond. The water in the pond was thick and black and poisonous, so that only unnamable invertebrates could live in it. (53-54)

The love/hate relationship between daughters and mothers is an indication of the ambiguity surrounding the position of women in West Indian society, where men "enjoy much greater social and sexual freedom" than women, and where men "are the focus of society's power relationships and occupy, in general, positions within it which inculcate concomitant attitudes of social and psychological authority."[5]

Judging from the stories written by West Indian women, the feelings of betrayal by the mother that begin at puberty reflect a growing sense of fear and distrust of the female body itself, emotions that are reinforced by the mother's warnings about sexual activity. Annie John despises "this young lady business" and feels a stranger in her own body (27). The mother in the first *River* story admonishes her daughter "to try to walk like a lady and not like the slut you are so bent on becoming" (3). A similar episode occurs in *Jane and Louisa Will Soon Come Home*, by Erna Brodber, which resembles the *River* stories in its subversion of linear development and chronological time. In this novel the narrator, Nellie Richmond, imagines her mother's response to the daughter's first sexual encounter: "Shame. You feel shame and you see your mother's face and you hear her scream and you feel the snail what she see making for your mouth. . . . You want to be a woman; now you have a man, you'll be like everybody else. You're normal now. Vomit and bear it" (28). The last sentence, which alludes to pregnancy and childbirth, suggests that a woman's biological nature will keep her trapped in a cycle of domestic drudgery, shut off from opportunities in the public realm: "Wash the white clothes on Monday and put them on the clothesline to dry" (Kincaid, *River* 3).

Although the "paradigm of male dominance" in West Indian society fails to account for the matriarchal power structure *within* the home (Murdoch 328), the youthful protagonists in these coming-of-age narratives require opportunities for achievement in the public domain. The dialogic interplay with the mother is no longer adequate; new voices enter the narratives as the protagonists discover a world outside the home.

The mothers in these stories by Kincaid and Brodber pass on to their daughters a profound sense of connectedness to history and to society. This revelation is not a message that the daughters are eager to hear. "Vomit and bear it." Know that you will be held accountable for your actions, which will have lasting repercussions in family life and the life of the community. With this sense of connectedness comes an overwhelming desire to escape. Escape can take the form of physical or psychological withdrawal: Annie's prolonged illness, Nellie's nervous breakdown. Self-imposed exile is another common response: Annie leaves her island home for school in England, Nellie spends time abroad studying.

Although Beka Lamb, Zee Edgell's protagonist in her novel by the same name, does not leave Belize within the time frame of the novel, she tells her grandmother that after graduation she will leave for distant lands. Having witnessed the "break down" of her best friend Toycie, who loses her reason and eventually her life as the result of an unplanned pregnancy, Beka begins to form a contingency plan of her own. Although Beka has experienced academic difficulties, which she compounds by lying to her parents, she knows that school is her only hope of escape from "the washing bowl underneath the house bottom." When the nuns at their Catholic school expel the pregnant Toycie, Beka realizes how vulnerable women are:

> There were no words ready for Beka to explain to her gran that, if, as she was beginning to suspect, her nurture was such that her life would probably break down, maybe in Toycie's way, she wanted it to happen in a far away corner where she could maybe pick up the pieces, glue them together and start all over again. (147)

Ironically, at the end of the novel, Granny Ivy admits to Beka that she herself was "caught" by "Toycie's first trouble . . . and I turned to rocking the cradle"

(170). But Beka takes comfort in the knowledge that Granny Ivy "didn't break down and die." Her grandmother is active in the public realm as a founding member of the People's Independence Party and thus serves as a role model for Beka.

Women learn at a very young age that there is "no alibi" for existence, that their "relation to life in all its aspects is one of intense participation" (Holquist 153). These novels remind us of "the more disturbing implications of being *fated* to the condition of dialogue," a condition that Michael Holquist stresses is not the "mindless pluralism" or "toothless carnivalism" that some of Bakhtin's less perceptive readers make it out to be. However, the challenges and responsibilities of dialogic interplay are not without their rewards, as is evidenced by those novels in which the protagonist's sense of self is eventually defined by her relation to the community in a mutually enriching symbiotic relationship.

In *Brown Girl, Brownstones,* by the Barbadian-American novelist Paule Marshall, Selina Boyce's love/hate relationship with her mother is intensified by the marital problems and incompatible temperaments of her parents: Deighton, who dreams of Barbados, and Silla, whose ambition to get ahead in the United States drives a wedge between her and her family. Selina eventually rejects her mother's values, refuses to participate in the Barbadian community association, and begins a clandestine affair with a man who is the antithesis of her mother. She also seeks acceptance in the world of her white school friends, only to be devastated when the mother of one of these friends comments in surprise: "you don't even act coloured. I mean, you speak so well and have such poise. And it's just wonderful how you've taken your race's natural talent for dancing and music and developed it" (288). This experience motivates Selina to seek identity "within the context of a specific black community rather than in reaction to a hostile white society" (Christian 104). She sees her reflection in the faces of the members of the Barbadian Association, "those myriad reflections and variations of her own dark face. And suddenly she admired their mystery. No, not mystery . . . but the mysterious source of endurance in them, and it was not only admiration but love she felt" (Marshall 302). Once Selina is able to identify with the Barbadian community, it is a short step to a partial reconciliation with her mother: "Everybody used to call me Deighton's Selina but they were wrong. Because you see I'm truly your child" (307).

Like the other novels of dialogic interplay, *Brown Girl, Brownstones* vacillates more than it progresses, and these moments of identity with the mother and the community are followed by the protagonist's realization that she must turn down a scholarship from the Barbadian Association, turn her back on Brooklyn and her mother, and seek "her own small truth that dimly envisioned a different world and a different way" (225). Selina has found the voice she has sought since childhood, when she saw herself as "a thin dark girl in galoshes without any power with words" (99). With this new voice she can gain access to the previously closed world of adults by engaging in dialogue with the community and the world beyond. The novel's openendedness reinforces the notion that this recognition is an ongoing process, not an isolated moment or epiphany. Selina is leaving, but she is not breaking her ties with her family and community: "She wanted, suddenly, to leave something with them." Pulling off one of her silver bangles, she tosses it behind her and listens to it strike the ground: "A frail sound in that utter silence" (310).

At the end of *Jane and Louisa Will Soon Come Home,* Nellie also finds her voice. Gay Wilentz observes: "Throughout the novel, the adult Nellie and the child Nellie clash; only in the final section, which shares the book's title, does a strong, clear voice emerge. This section is Nellie's generational, historical re-counting of her family's and her nation's past" (273). Through the healing pow-ers of her Rastafarian friend Baba, Nellie breaks out of the protective kumbla that her family has woven around her, a cocoon consisting of middle-class pre-tensions, pride in their white progenitor, and Eurocentric values. In the final section of the novel, Nellie opens a dialogue between the present and the past, the living and the dead; between standard Jamaican English and Creole; between Anglo-European traditions and Afro-Jamaican folk culture. Because of the loop-ing, non-linear structure of the novel, Nellie's reconciliation with her family and her nation is foreshadowed in section two when, during her six-week convales-cence from a nervous breakdown, she has a dream or a vision: "Last night I let myself into a new world. I simply walked in." This world takes shape in the way pieces of colored glass create images in a kaleidoscope: "I saw them stand still. They were people. I had sensed them but I could still not discern faces or limbs." When morning comes, Nellie is on the road to recovery: "I was no longer alone. Baba had settled me with my people" (75-77).

Annie John has a similar healing experience while under the care of her grandmother Ma Chess, an obeah woman. But Annie's recovery coincides with her realization that she wants nothing so much as to leave Antigua. Having pro-gressed through a series of interactions with female figures—her mother Annie, her friend Gwen, the Red Girl, and Ma Chess—Annie longs to take her place in the world beyond the Caribbean, so she departs for England where she will study nursing. Her failure to establish a meaningful connection with the West Indian community appears to weight on her mind, for exhilaration at the thought of leaving alternates with dread: "my heart swelled with a great gladness as the words 'I shall never see this again' spilled out inside me. But then, just as quickly, my heart shriveled up and the words 'I shall never see this place again' stabbed at me. I don't know what stopped me from falling in a heap at my par-ents' feet" (145).

The narrator in *At the Bottom of the River* moves closer than Annie John toward identity with the community. Although she covets "the rocks and the mountains their silence," she emerges from her "pit," as Nellie broke from the protective kumbla, and sees about her the accouterments of daily life:

a bowl of ripe fruit, a bottle of milk, a flute made of wood, the clothes that I will wear. And as I see these things in the light of the lamp, all perishable and transient, how bound up I know I am to all that is human endeavor, to all that is past and to all that shall be, to all that shall be lost and leave no trace. I claim these things then—mine—and now feel myself grow solid and complete, my name filling up my mouth. (82)

The speaker turns, albeit reluctantly, from the seductive silence of the non-human realm and finds her voice and identity in the dialogue of human endeavor. She has discovered that existence and activity are synonymous, and even passivity is "the activity of choosing to be passive" (Holquist 153).

For Beka Lamb, detachment is not an option. Her world is so dense and textured that every day calls for new adjustments. The novel *Beka Lamb* is a multivoiced narrative that is layered with historical, social, and cultural implications which go beyond the immediate conflicts between Beka and her family. The story unfolds in Belize at a time when the former colony was reassessing its role in relation to Great Britain and the islands of the West Indies, as well as Guatemala and the rest of Central America. The variety and complexity of life in postwar Belize present the young protagonist with a multitude of potential responses. The self that defines itself in relation to this multi-cultural environment must be an active participant in life. When Beka's friend Toycie is expelled from school because she is pregnant, Beka—like Annie John, Nellie Richmond and Selina Boyce—feels betrayed by gender. She too experiences a breakdown, a prolonged period of mourning for her beloved friend, and she longs to escape from her situation by traveling to distant lands. But Beka finds the strength to go on, and in the process she makes an important discovery about herself and her country. Beka tells Sister Gabriela, the teacher who believes in Beka's intelligence and creative ability: "Sometimes I feel bruk down just like my own country, Sister. I start all right but then I drift for the longest while." The wise sister advises Beka:

> You must go as far as the limitations of your life will allow. Find a way to do what you can, even though things seem to be crashing all around you. Sometimes they are not breaking down at all, sometimes things are taking a different shape. Try to recognize the pattern even if it is one you don't like, then maybe you can do something about it. (116)

Like Beka, Belize came through this time of discord prior to independence from Great Britain with a renewed sense of identity and purpose. The key for Beka and Belize was the ability to accommodate a plurality of voices and relations.

The connection between Beka's development and that of Belize is significant. Bakhtin singles out the *Bildungsroman* for special praise because the protagonist's "individual emergence is inseparably linked to historical emergence. . . . He emerges *along with the world* and he reflects the historical emergence of the world itself. . . . It is as though the very foundations of the world are changing, and man must change along with them" (*The Bildungsroman*" 23-4). For writers from Caribbean countries recently emerged from colonial dependency on Great Britain, the foundations of the world truly are changing. Beka's father, concerned that Guatemala has designs on Belize, tells his daughter that "bad as it is, the British brand of colonialism isn't the worst we could have" (*Beka Lamb* 7). Beka, however, is frustrated and angered by the various "claims" to Belize: "Guatemala claims Belize from Britain through rights inherited from Spain, and Spain got rights from the Pope, and who are we going to get rights from?" (36). The struggle against British colonial rule, the social problems linked to vestiges of slavery, and the neocolonial threat from the United States are themes that inform these novels by Caribbean women, and their protagonists are connected to history to an extent that Bakhtin could probably not have foreseen.

These novels exist, therefore, in a dialogic relationship with the male *Bildungsroman* and fulfill Bakhtin's vision of that genre's potential. They take what is of value from the adventure or quest plot, but they avoid the excesses of Romantic individualism by cultivating the "connection-paradigm" favored by such writers as Maria Edgeworth and Kathryn Lasky.[6] Kincaid, Brodber, Edgell, and Marshall build upon the efforts of Frances Burney, Charlotte Brontë, Jane Austen, and George Eliot, who opened a space within the *Bildungsroman* "for confusion, complaint, critique, and possibly compensation regarding issues of female development" (Fraiman 141). But Annie John, Nellie Richmond, Beka Lamb, and Selina Boyce are not bound by the "marriage plot" or other bourgeois conventions that circumscribed the middle-class English woman's life in previous centuries. Like the developing nations they call home, these young women are taking control of their destinies, and their authors are reinventing the novel of development to accommodate the needs and demands of women on the brink of a new century.

Notes

1. The novels and stories I discuss vary greatly in degree of difficulty. She found *Annie John* and especially *Beka Lamb* to be accessible to her high school and junior high school students. *Brown Girl, Brownstones*, like *Annie John*, traces the development of the protagonist from childhood to early adulthood and as a result, the vocabulary and situations in both novels are better suited to senior high school and college students than to younger students. *At the Bottom of the River* and *Jane and Louisa Will Soon Come Home* would be beyond the reach of many young adults because of the experimental techniques of these works.

2. According to Jeffrey L. Sammons, "the concept of Bildung is intensely bourgeois; it carries with it many assumptions about the autonomy and relative integrity of the self," assumptions that have become increasingly difficult to sustain in the modern world (42). As the term Bildungsroman loses touch with its bourgeois humanistic roots and is applied to novels with radically different historical and ideological parameters, Sammons argues, it becomes less useful as a tool in genre studies.

3. For example, although it could be argued that Joyce's *A Portrait of the Artist as a Young Man* contains some dialogic elements, the following passage from the novel indicates that Stephen Dedalus's most significant discovery is himself as Byronic hero, not "the other" in any guise: "He was alone. He was unheeded, happy and near to the wild heart of life. He was alone and young and willful and wildhearted, and amid a waste of wild air and brackish waters and the seaharvest of shells and tangle and veiled grey sunlight and gayclad lightclad figures, of children and girls and voices childish and girlish in the air" (171).

4. Myers uses this expression in an article on the eighteenth-century stories of female development written by Maria Edgeworth, of which Myers says: "Their

dialogic interplay of child and adult, daughter and mother, constitutes a double-voiced narrative of some subtlety and considerable literary moment" (68).
5. Edith Clark, *My Mother Who Fathered Me* (London: Allen, 1972), 104-106, paraphrased in Murdoch (328).
6. For a discussion of Kathryn Lasky's contribution to the female novel of development, see Sibel Erol.

Works Cited

Abel, Elizabeth, Marianne Hirsch, and Elizabeth Langland, eds. Introduction. *The Voyage In: Fictions of Female Development*. Hanover, NH: University Press of New England, 1983.

Bakhtin, Mikhail M. "The *Bildungsroman* and Its Significance in the History of Realism (Toward a Historical Typology of the Novel)." *Speech Genres and the Other Late Essays*. University of Texas Press Slavic Series 8. Trans. Vern W. McGee. Ed. Caryl Emerson and Michael Holquist. 1986. Austin: University of Texas Press, 1992.

———. *Problems of Dostoevsky's Poetics*. Ed. and trans. Caryl Emerson. 1984. Minneapolis: University of Minnesota Press, 1989.

Brodber, Erna. *Jane and Louisa Will Soon Come Home*. London: New Beacon, 1980.

Christian, Barbara. *Black Feminist Criticism: Perspectives on Black Women Writers*. New York: Pergamon, 1985.

Edgell, Zee. *Beka Lamb*. London: Heinemann, 1982.

Erol, Sibel. "*Beyond the Divide:* Lasky's Feminist Revision of the Westward Journey." *Children's Literature Association Quarterly* 17.1 (1992): 5-8.

Fraiman, Susan. *Unbecoming Women: British Women Writers and the Novels of Development*. New York: Columbia University Press, 1993.

Heilbrun, Carolyn G. *Writing a Woman's Life*. New York: Ballantine, 1988.

Holquist, Michael. *Bakhtin and His World*. New York: Routledge, 1990.

Joyce, James. *A Portrait of the Artist as a Young Man: Text, Criticism, and Notes*. Ed. Chester G. Anderson. 1977. New York: Penguin, 1982.

Kincaid, Jamaica. *Annie John*. 1983. New York: NAL/Plume, 1985.

———. *At the Bottom of the River*. New York: Aventura/Vintage, 1985.

Marshall, Paule. *Brown Girl, Brownstones*. 1959. New York: Feminist Press, 1981.

Morris, Ann R. and Margaret M. Dunn. "'The Bloodstream of Our Inheritance': Female Identity and the Caribbean Mothers'-Land." *Motherlands: Black Women's Writing from Africa, the Caribbean and South Asia*. Ed. Susheila Nasta. New Brunswick, NJ: Rutgers University Press, 1992.

Murdoch, H. Adlai. "Severing the (M)other Connection: The Representation of Cultural Identity in Jamaica Kincaid's *Annie John*." *Callaloo* 13.2 (1990): 325-40.

Myers, Mitzi. "The Dilemmas of Gender as Double-Voiced Narrative; or, Maria Edgeworth Mothers the Bildungsroman." *The Idea of the Novel in the Eighteenth Century*. Ed. Robert W. Uphaus. East Lansing, MI: Colleagues Press, 1988.

Natov, Roni. "Mothers and Daughters: Jamaica Kincaid's Pre-Oedipal Narrative." *Children's Literature* 18 (1990): 1-16.

Sammons, Jeffrey L. "The Bildungsroman for Nonspecialists: An Attempt at Clarification." *Reflection and Action: Essays on the Bildungsroman*. Ed. James Hardin. Columbia, SC: University of South Carolina Press, 1991.

Shea, Renee Hausmann. "Gilligan's 'Crisis of Connections': Contemporary Caribbean Women Writers." *English Journal* 81.4 (1992): 36-41.

Wilentz, Gay. "English Is a Foreign Anguish: Caribbean Writers and the Disruption of the Colonial Canon." *Decolonizing Tradition: New Views of Twentieth-Century "British" Literary Canons*. Ed. Karen R. Lawrence. Urbana and Chicago: University of Illinois Press, 1992.

The Novel of Relational Autonomy:
West Indian Women Writers and the
Evolution of Genre

The coming-of-age novel by West Indian women writers represents an important development in the evolution of the novel as genre. Writers such as Jamaica Kincaid, Zee Edgell, Michelle Cliff and Merle Collins, to mention just a few, have not only made important contributions to the novel of adolescence, but they have challenged the very concept of development, questioning the assumptions that underlie both the male *Bildungsroman* or quest plot and the female marriage or courtship plot. Furthermore, they have provided an alternative to these limited and limiting narrative models.

For contemporary women writers from developing nations, the dichotomy suggested by these narrative models between male and female life experiences is problematic. Additionally, the historical and cultural roots of the *Bildungsroman* and the courtship novel in nineteenth-century bourgeois European society are philosophically incompatible with the depiction of characters whose existence is premised on hundreds of years of oppression and exploitation by those same European societies. Maria Helena Lima argues persuasively that Cliff and Collins "expose the complexity of the contradictions within generic conventions," but she also maintains that the *Bildungsroman* survives as a genre, though expanded and transformed: "The genre's survival might in itself mark the victory of the colonizer but its transformation in countries attempting decolonization offers provisional rewriting of origin and identity, rhetorical configurations that will undergo further change as the process of recovery continues" (35-6). It is my contention that the novel of development has undergone such a radical transformation in the hands of West Indian women writers that it is no longer appropriate to refer to it as *Bildungsroman*.[1] What is needed is a new term, one that is free from the cultural and historical implications of the German word, a term that acknowledges the attempt of these writers to subvert gender-based dichotomies. Furthermore, by naming this literary phenomenon I hope to draw attention to its importance, for the novels that are being written by West Indian women represent the culmination of the genre itself as envisioned by Mikhail Bakhtin.

The novel, for Bakhtin, "is the characteristic text of a particular stage in the history of consciousness not because it marks the self's discovery of itself, but because it manifests the self's discovery of the other" (Holquist 75). The *Bildungsroman* epitomized the novel as a genre for Bakhtin because in it the protagonist "emerges *along with the world* and he reflects the historical emergence of the world itself" (Bakhtin 23). However, the *Bildungsroman* depended on Romantic notions of individualism and the self's autonomy, which seriously limited the protagonist's efforts to reach beyond himself toward a recognition of "the other." Equally problematic is the fact that the *Bildungsroman* failed to acknowledge the maturational experiences of women, and efforts since the nine-teenth century to establish a distinctive female model of development—from Jane Austen's novels of courtship and marriage to the male-separation/female-connection paradigms of Nancy Chodorow and Carol Gilligan—remain prob-lematic, according to Susan Fraiman, because they continue to marginalize women by remaining "too obligingly within the given contours of 'women's culture,' neglecting the troubling appeal and predominance of the *Bildungsro-man* for female figures" (143-4).[2]

In *Reflections on Gender and Science*, Evelyn Fox Keller provides insight into the psychological and historical implications of the autonomy/relatedness dichotomy:

> My argument is not simply that the dream of a completely objective science is in principle unrealizable, but that it contains precisely what it rejects: the vivid traces of a reflected self image. The objectivist illusion reflects back an image of self as autonomous and objectified: an image of individuals unto themselves, severed from the outside world of other objects (animate as well as inanimate) and simultaneously from their own subjectivity. (70)

Keller suggests that we replace the static notion of autonomy, which entails con-trol and domination, with a dynamic and flexible autonomy that emphasizes relatedness, not at the expense of delineation, but rather through an "exquisite balancing act" between desire for independence and the longing for intimacy (100). She also rejects "the cultural definition of male and female as polar oppo-sites, the one premised on difference and the other on similarity," calling instead for "the development of dynamic autonomy for both sexes" (107).

Borrowing from Keller, I have coined the term "novel of relational auton-omy" to describe the novels of development by West Indian women writers. In these novels, the female protagonists are defined from birth by their connection to others, yet their individuality is not compromised by intimacy; rather it is enhanced by human contact. The novel unfolds as the protean "other" takes on a variety of shapes: mother, friend, lover, community. These narratives trace the expansion of the protagonist's consciousness as she recognizes and acknowl-edges the complexity of the world, defining herself in relation to it. This recog-nition is an ongoing process, not an isolated moment: as she grows in self-awareness, her knowledge of the world expands. The novel of relational auton-omy is thus the culmination of Bakhtin's vision of the novel as genre, for in it consciousness achieves the dialogic awareness that existed only in nascent form in the *Bildungsroman*.

The earliest manifestation of relational autonomy occurs between daughters and mothers, and it intensifies during adolescence.[3] In novels by Jamaica Kin-caid, Paule Marshall, Erna Brodber and many other women writers from the Anglophone Caribbean, the love/hate relationship between daughters and moth-ers is an indication of the ambiguity surrounding the position of women in West Indian society. The feelings of betrayal by the mother that begin at puberty re-flect a growing sense of fear and distrust of the female body, emotions that are reinforced by the mother's warnings against sexual activity. Gradually the daughter transfers the focus of her affection from her mother to her female friends. In this, the second stage of development of relational autonomy, the youthful protagonist begins to require opportunities for achievement and recognition in the public domain. New voices enter the narrative as the protagonist discovers a world outside the home. This paper will examine novels in which a post-adolescent female protagonist (viewed as a composite of characters from several novels) moves beyond the nuclear family into the realm of like-minded young women, and from there progresses—or attempts to progress—toward an engagement with the larger society through political involvement.

Female Friendships and Relational Autonomy

Karen Schultz, citing Carol Gilligan, maintains that the literature of psychology has largely ignored the importance of friendship because "friendship is more crucial to women than to men. Our psychology has been a male psychology, with women's specific features fitted in as pathological variants" (21). However, friendship between female characters in West Indian novels is one of the primary indicators of the protagonist's development. "We repeat and resolve crucial psychological conflicts in the changing relationships we make with friends. Friendships raise and resolve issues of nurturance and neediness, competition and cooperation, autonomy and dependency" (Schultz 19). A brief look at novels by Jamaica Kincaid and Zee Edgell will reveal how female friendships can facilitate the difficult balance between individuation and relatedness, enabling the protagonists to evolve toward relational autonomy through dialogic interaction with others. Conversely, the refusal or inability of the protagonist to relax the boundary between self and other is a gauge of the character's fear that relatedness will jeopardize her quest for independence and differentiation, which is the case in Kincaid's first novel, *Annie John*.

As mother and daughter in *Annie John* grow further apart, the adolescent narrator transfers much of her intense love to two girls, first to proper Gweneth Joseph and then to the wild, unwashed "Red Girl." The second friendship is notable for its sadomasochistic elements. When the girls meet secretly, since Annie's mother would not approve, the Red Girl pinches Annie until she cries, then kisses the sore spots. Annie exclaims:

> Oh, the sensation was delicious—the combination of pinches and kisses. And so wonderful we found it that, almost every time we met, pinching by her, followed by tears from me, followed by kisses from her were the order of the day. I stopped wondering why all the girls whom I had mistreated and abandoned followed me around with looks of love and adoration on their faces. (63)

"Overt sadism," according to Evelyn Fox Keller, "merely exhibits in pure form a phenomenon that is pandemic in human psychology: the appetite for domination, whether sexual or nonsexual. . . . In short, domination is a response to the dangers of another's powerlessness evoked by one's own failure of differentiation and autonomy" (105-6). The sadomasochistic element in Annie's relationship with other girls indicates that she has not achieved relational autonomy.

Rather than dynamic exchange, we have an endless regression of mirror images: Annie loves the very qualities in the Red Girl that she, Annie, exhibits in her relationships with other girls and that she perceives, wrongly or rightly, in her mother's treatment of her. Unable or unwilling to resolve conflicting feelings of love and hatred toward her mother, torn by a longing to submit and a need to rebel, Annie continues to reenact this pre-oedipal drama with her female friends.[4] When Annie prepares to leave Antigua at the end of the novel, to study nursing in England, exhilaration at the thought of escape alternates with dread, and she departs with her need for relationship still at war with her desire for autonomy.

Kincaid's second novel, *Lucy*, picks up roughly where *Annie John* ended. Although the protagonists have different names and situations (Lucy is an au pair in the United States), there are striking similarities. Lucy is nineteen years old and deeply conflicted regarding her mother, whose letters she refuses to open: "I knew that if I read only one, I would die from longing for her" (91). When Annie departed Antigua, her mother said, "It doesn't matter what you do or where you go, I'll always be your mother and this will always be your home" (147). Lucy recalls her mother's parting words: "You can run away, but you cannot escape the fact that I am your mother, my blood runs in you, I carried you for nine months inside me." Lucy reflects: "How else was I to take such a statement but as a sentence for life in a prison whose bars were stronger than any iron imaginable?" Lucy's identification with her mother is complete—"I was not like my mother—I was my mother" (90)—and her inability to establish a relationship with her mother based on dynamic, interactive autonomy blights her friendships.

When Mariah, the wealthy white American woman for whom Lucy works, attempts to get closer to Lucy, she resists largely because she has conflated Mariah and her mother: "I began to feel like a dog on a leash, a long leash but a leash all the same. Mariah was like a mother to me, a good mother" (110).[5] Throughout the novel, Lucy uses the force of her anger and intelligence to keep people at a distance: "I was alone in the world. It was not a small accomplishment. I thought I would die doing it. I was not happy, but that seemed too much to ask" (161). Because Lucy attributes godlike powers to her mother, she casts herself in the role of Lucifer: "Lucy, a girl's name for Lucifer. That my mother would have found me devil-like did not surprise me, for I often thought of her as god-like, and are not the children of the gods devils?" (153). A prisoner of her regressive longing for pre-adolescent union with her mother, Lucy adopts a stance of static autonomy and Romantic individualism. Unable to maintain that delicate balance between independence and intimacy, Lucy chooses isolation.

Jamaica Kincaid writes novels of nearly tragic proportions. Her protagonists' anger and pride prevent them from accepting others—their mothers, friends, lovers, and those who would like to be their friends and lovers. In her novels of development, relational autonomy is the elusive goal, the ever-present but never fully realized alternative to the brittle, brilliant cynicism of her protagonists.

In Zee Edgell's first novel, *Beka Lamb*, the vision of adolescent development is not without its tragic elements, but ultimately it is a hopeful and expansive rendering of life in Belize, then British Honduras, in the decades preceding the country's independence from England. In *Beka Lamb*, the young protagonist attempts to come to terms with the death of her best friend, Toycie, after an unplanned pregnancy results in Toycie's expulsion from the Catholic school where both girls are students. Education was the only means of escape for Toycie from grinding, degrading poverty. The loss of her prospects weakens Toycie's hold on reality, leading to a suicide attempt, a miscarriage, and finally death.

The story takes place in the 1950s against a background of political unrest caused by British Honduras' struggle for independence from England, its fear of intervention from neighboring Guatemala, and numerous social problems that plague the colony's multi-racial population. Toycie and Beka seek, through education, to escape the fate of most Creole women in Belize City: the washing bowl underneath the house bottom, in the swampy yard where mosquitoes and the stench from the latrine make the grueling work of boiling the white clothes nearly unbearable (22). Despite a three-year difference in age (Beka is fourteen, Toycie seventeen), the young women are united by their ambition: "Toycie and Beka were different on the street where economic necessity forced many Creole girls to leave school after elementary education to help at home, work in shops and stores as salesladies or take jobs as domestic servants in the houses of those who could afford such help" (34). Toycie is the better student, but she lacks Beka's tenacity and strength. Beka's fear of failure, of breaking down "just like [her] country," is the challenge she must meet, especially when Toycie withdraws into madness, leaving Beka to fend for herself without the optimism, support and encouragement that Toycie had always provided.

Ironically, the loss of Toycie brings out the best in Beka. According to Karen Schultz, "while women's friendships can enhance development, they can also discourage it. Women often bond through sharing problems rather than successes. Fear of friends' envy inhibits competition and ambition among women. Women's nurturance of one another is often over-protective, supporting weakness instead of strength" (23). While Toycie was alive, Beka seemed content to be the poor student, the dishonest daughter who lied rather than admit she had flunked her first form, the foil to Toycie's considerable achievements. When Toycie becomes pregnant, their roles are suddenly reversed. Beka must be the strong one. She tells Toycie: "I'll help you if it's a baby, Toycie. We'll live together when I leave school and raise it as best we can, and if it's a girl, we'll explain everything carefully about everything so that her life doesn't break down that way. And if it's a boy, we'll do the same" (109). Toycie will not be consoled; she has lost her desire to live. But after Toycie's death, Beka finds consolation "by working at something beyond her natural capacity. Instead of finding the work irksome, as she once would have done, she found she enjoyed it; there was satisfaction in the challenge and she was growing less dependent on the family's praise to make her feel whole" (151). When Beka wins an essay contest at St. Cecilia's Academy, she learns that even a small success can help to stave off panic and fear, can enable her to look back on the events of the recent past and see that in her pain and anguish something new was taking shape. The novel ends when Beka feels that her private wake for Toycie has run its course: "Her watch-night for Toycie was over and she felt released—there was need no more for guilt or grief over a mourning postponed" (171).

Beka has achieved a degree of autonomy, but not at the expense of empathy and cooperation. Her relationships with her parents and grandmother are strengthened by her independence and sense of accomplishment. For Beka, coming of age entails a redefinition of herself in relation to her family, her friend, and her community. Beka's dream of someday going into politics and helping her country to deal with its many problems is one step closer by the end of the novel.

An important aspect of development in novels by West Indian women is the fact that it is an ongoing process; relational autonomy is not something achieved at one point in life but a continuing evolution of consciousness. For this reason, many writers trace the development of female protagonists through the stages of a women's life. Jamaica Kincaid has given us adolescent Annie John, the young adult, Lucy Josephine Potter, and most recently the narrator of *The Autobiography of My Mother*, Xuela Claudette Richardson, who is a woman in her seventies. Barbadian-American Paule Marshall has taken us from the adolescence of Selina Boyce in *Brown Girl, Brownstones* to Avey Johnson's voyage to self-discovery at age sixty-four in *Praisesong for the Widow*. Similarly, in Zee Edgell's second novel, *In Times Like These*, we meet Pavana Leslie, a Belizean woman in her early thirties whose life "broke down" like Toycie's, but did so twelve years before the events of the novel, while she was a student in London, in a better position to take control of her life as a single mother and provide for the twins when they were born. When Beka imagines "that her life would probably break down, probably in Toycie's way," she decides that if it did, "she wanted it to happen in a far away corner where she could maybe pick up the pieces, glue them togther and start all over again" (147). That is precisely what has happened to Pavana. When she returns in 1981 to Belize City on the eve of Independence, to take a job in the government, we see a woman who is not broken by life but rather strengthened by adversity, a woman whose dynamic and flexible autonomy enhances her relationships with her family, her friends, and her nation.

The Protagonist and Her World Come of Age

Novels that depict the protagonist's entrance into the political life of her nation fulfill the potential that Bakhtin saw in the *Bildungsroman* for personal development to reflect historical emergence. However, for reasons already mentioned regarding the psychological limitations and historical assumptions embedded in the term *Bildungsroman*, it's even less appropriate when applied to novels such as Edgell's *In Times Like These*, Michelle Cliff's *Abeng* and *No Telephone to Heaven*, and Merle Collins's *Angel* and *The Colour of Forgetting*. In these novels, the protagonist strives for relational autonomy with her nation, her race, the present as well as past and future generations. These novels are multi-voiced, and in Collins's narratives even the term "protagonist" appears anachronistic.

Because relational autonomy is an ongoing process, the stages overlap. Dialogic relationships with the mother and close female friends do not simply yield to the demands of career and community; rather, the threads of these early relationships form a part of the larger pattern that emerges with the protagonist's increasing age and maturity. The later stages of relational autonomy place the early experiences in perspective, as the protagonist becomes aware of her place in history. This "dialogue of chronotypes" (Gary Saul Morson quoted in Burton 48) reflects Bakhtin's "idea of multiple, interrelated senses of time, not merely in the same historical era, but also with respect to the same text: often it is the struggle or dialogue between them that animates the narrative" (Burton 46). These West Indian novels are animated by dialogue between the past and present lives of the protagonists, between younger and older generations, and between conflicting accounts of historical events. According to Michael Valdez Moses,

> the lack of any strict division among the spheres of art, academics, and politics within much of the Third World leads us to question whether the designation of literary history as a purely *academic* problem is universally valid, rather than historically contingent upon and politically delimited by the norms of Western liberal democratic regimes. In fact, if one does not insist on disciplinary boundaries between the practices of literary history and literary art, one begins to discover that many poems, plays, and novels from the Third World are actively engaged in the construction of literary history. (208-9)

In the novels in question, focusing as they do on political tensions experienced by Belize, Jamaica, Grenada, and the mythical islands of Paz and Eden, as they emerge from colonial domination during the second half of the twentieth century, literary history is not "a mere museum piece" but rather an active engagement fraught with "challenge and danger" (Moses 212).

Challenge and danger await Pavana Leslie, the protagonist in Zee Edgell's second novel, *In Times Like These*, when she steps off the plane in Belize City. The city and the country are in a state of profound unrest. As Independence Day approaches, distrust and hostility surface at all levels of Belizean society. Rumors fly, fed by the insecurity of the populace: "Belizeans had lived with the threat of a 'Guatemala take-over' for so long that it was quite easy for them to instantly hear the clump, clump, scrape, scrape of soldiers' boots, see the guns, feel the bullets and watch their homes burst into flames" (47). The government's plan to resolve the Anglo-Guatemalan dispute over Belize is seen as betrayal, and the people take their complaints to the streets in the form of riots and, on March 31, 1981, a nationwide strike.

Pavana learns that her appointment to a position in the Ministry of Community Development, heading up a unit on Women and Development, was bitterly opposed by certain cabinet members. Her efforts to improve the condition of poor women in rural Belize and to give them a voice in the public arena are thwarted by government officials who feel that Pavana is presenting the Belizean leadership in a negative light. Political infighting and even sabotage in her unit frustrate Pavana at every turn. On a more personal level, she finds herself caught between the conflicting political visions of two former friends, men she had known during her university days in London. When Stoner Bennett modified his passionate black power rhetoric to curry favor in Belize's racially diverse society, he lost touch with the grass roots movement. Now he lives primarily to plague his nemesis Alex Abrams, whose flirtation with socialism years ago while studying in London, if exposed by Stoner, could cost Alex his position within Belize's ruling party. Alex has abandoned his youthful idealism, and his attempt to effect a compromise between England and Guatemala has placed him in an awkward position with regard to his fellow Belizeans. After Alex delivers a speech in support of "law and order," Pavana observes "the group of men carrying Alex, waving and bowing to supporters screaming him name, although the vast majority of spectators lining the streets watched silently, knowing his speech had been less than honest, and his talk had been directed at the already converted and to his party's hard liners. If a hero's function is to inspire people to be better, to do better, what had Alex become in their eyes?" (271). When Pavana reveals that her twelve-year-old twins are Alex's children, she unwittingly places them in harm's way, for the children becomes pawns in the political battle between Alex's hard liners and Stoner's left-wing Action Committee. The violence escalates, and Alex is killed by his own thugs when he attempts to save Stoner's life.

As the events of the novel unfold, it becomes clear that there are no easy solutions, no clear-cut choices between right and wrong, good and evil. Some of the most significant observations, such as the one above regarding Alex in the eyes of the people, are framed as questions without answers. When Pavana and Alex discuss the failure of both the black power and socialist ideologies of their student days to gain support back home in Belize, she asks: "Maybe it was also because the ideologies of both factions were imported, alien to Belizean values, traditions and all that?" (141). Pavana fears that her own feminist agenda for the Women and Development unit "is another new idea, another importation and" (141). Unanswered questions and unfinished sentences rhetorically reinforce the dilemma facing this developing nation on the eve of Independence. Pavana's refusal to succumb to despair and cynicism is an indication of her maturity, of the degree to which she has achieved relational autonomy. Ultimately it is Pavana, rather than Stoner or Alex, who emerges as Belize's best hope for the future. Unlike the men, Pavana is not wedded to an ideology or hungry for power. She relies on cooperation rather than confrontation in her efforts to improve the living conditions for poor Belizean women.

While Edgell's novel provides a literary account of a pivotal moment in the history of Belize, in *Abeng* and *No Telephone to Heaven* Michelle Cliff attempts to recover the unwritten history of Jamaica's colonial past. According to Michael Valdez Moses, "Revisionism is only one goal of much contemporary Third World fiction. A significant number of works engage in the literary historical task of consolidating and promoting an indigenous or non-European literary tradition" (210). Clare Savage, the protagonist in both of Cliff's novels, is the embodiment of Jamaica's past. A light-skinned descendent of slave owners and slaves, the colonizer and the colonized, Clare is described as an "albino gorilla" who feels very little "except a vague dread that she belongs nowhere. . . . Time passes. The longing for tribe surfaces. Unmistakable" (*NTTH* 91). The first novel, *Abeng*, recounts Clare's childhood years in Jamaica, while *No Telephone to Heaven* picks up in 1960, when fourteen-year-old Clare and her family move to New York City, and ends with her violent death at age thirty-five. Critics frequently point out the parallels between Clare's life and that of Antoinette/Bertha, the while Creole protagonist in *Wide Sargasso Sea*. Belinda Edmondson describes Clare's death in a failed guerrilla raid on an American movie set in Jamaica as an act "of conscious resistance, though she, like Bertha, dies in the act of resisting" (185). Clare Savage has indeed found her niche in Jamaica's history, but as in the case of *Wide Sargasso Sea*, I would argue that the violent death of this light-skinned Creole woman is less a conscious decision than the culmination of grim historical forces that were set in motion with Clare's great-great-grandfather, James Edward Constable Savage, who reacted to the imminent emancipation of Jamaica's slaves by setting fire to the slave quarters on his property, killing most of the inhabitants (*Abeng* 40).

Clare's involvement with the communist guerrilla group is the final stage of her life-long quest to establish a connection with the rural black community, which is her maternal heritage, a heritage that her white father has endeavored to erase. In *NTTH*, Clare turns her grandmother's "ruinate" property in St. Elizabeth over to the rebels, reasoning rather naively that because her grandmother and mother "believed in using the land to feed people," they must have been communists and would therefore approve of her actions. However, Clare's vilification of her father and elevation of her mother and grandmother to near mythic proportions (black women in both novels are linked metaphorically to the Maroon leader Nanny), the narratives do not support this reductive binary structure. For instance, when Clare was still a young girl, it was her mother, Kitty, who abandoned her in New York and returned to Jamaica with the younger (and darker-skinned) daughter, leaving Clare in the care of her father, Boy. And in *Abeng* we witness the scene, after Clare has accidentally shot and killed her grandmother's bull, when Miss Mattie condemns her granddaughter to the condition of exile that plagues the younger woman for the remainder of her life:

> [Miss Mattie] made herself glad that she would see the last of her eldest granddaughter for a time. She did not think that this exile might teach Clare a lesson—that her granddaughter might mend her ways once punished by a period of banishment. Miss Mattie had made a judgment—that Clare was only what she appeared to be; not of Miss Mattie at all, but of Boy's side of the family. The child had no sense of country. He should be the one to punish his daughter; the girl was his child after all. (145)

Perhaps Miss Mattie's decision to leave her property to Clare was a gesture of atonement for the swiftness and severity of her judgment in this matter.

In *NTTH*, the African-American man named Bobby, who becomes Clare's lover in England, provides insight into Clare's dilemma regarding Boy and Kitty. Kitty's family blames her death from a brain hemorrhage on Boy, despite the fact that she ignored the warning signs and refused to see a doctor. When Clare tells Bobby that she did not visit her mother's grave for fear of upsetting her mother's relatives, he responds: "Baby, you afflicted with something rare." Why can't she confront her aunt and uncle, Bobby asks, and tell them "you people full of shit, my father didn't kill nobody?" But like her mother's relatives, Clare holds her father accountable, believing that his decision to migrate to the United States set in motion the series of events that led to Kitty's death. Bobby urges Clare "to get to the place where you are apart from your mother, your father, while still being a part of them. For they made you, like it or not" (152-3). Bobby is urging Clare toward relational autonomy—being "apart from" while still "a part of"—but Clare has accepted her role as sacrificial Aztec princess, her father's term of endearment for his daughter, "golden in the sun," when she was a young child: "'Clare, you would have certainly been a choice for sacrifice—you know the Aztecs slaughtered their most beautiful virgins and drank their blood.' It did not occur to Clare to question her father's reading of history—a world view in which she would have been chosen for divine slaughter" (*Abeng* 10). Clare's vision of herself as sacrificial lamb predisposes her for seduction by the imported revolutionary rhetoric of the female guerrilla leader. While the rebels in the house above are hatching their plans at attack the American movie set, Clare slithers under her grandmother's house with the webs of poisonous spiders, rat droppings, and scorpions. In this womb/tomb she finds solace in regressive, almost infantile contemplation of the remnants of her mother's childhood—schoolbooks, dolls, and other toys. Her death by gunfire a short time later fulfills her father's prediction for his golden child.

In a review of the movie version of *Wide Sargasso Sea*, Cliff writes: "I emerged from a world that deserved to die, one that had changed little from the time of *Wide Sargasso Sea* to the time of my girlhood. But it was never a simple world. The world of the Caribbean has no center and no outward edge. Its customs and travails, its dangers and its gifts, forge extraordinary creatures" (78). Clare Savage is one of those extraordinary creatures. Her abortion (like Anna Morgan's in *Voyage in the Dark*) and subsequent sterility mark the end of her father's line; her violent death links her to her mother's people, the African slaves who "ate dirt, Kitty told her, when this life became too much for them" (*NTTH* 174). According to a Jamaican proverb, "no one black dies a natural death" (*NTTH* 181). Clare's most unnatural death closes the book on the Savage family's colonial past and the atrocities of her great-great-grandfather, and reunites her with her mother's tribe after a lifetime of exile.

In an essay in which she compares *NTTH* to Merle Collins's *Angel*, Maria Helena Lima describes Cliff's novel as "a tragically individualist tale" which, "despite its critique of the People's National Party (PNP) does not want to bring Jamaicans together for another experiment in democratic socialism" (42, 37). *Angel*, on the other hand, is seen by Lima as "a call to arms," as a revolutionary "reconceptualization of the *Bildungsroman*" that combines "the individual novel of formation" with "the collectivity of the *testimonio*" (43). Lima's definition of the *testimonio* suggests a degree of relational autonomy unprecedented in the novel as genre, which makes me question her continued dependence on the term *Bildungsroman.* While Collins's first novel continues to affirm the individual subject in the protagonist Angel McAllister, her second novel, *The Colour of Forgetting,* is an even more radical departure from the *Bildungsroman* in that it is difficult to speak of a protagonist except as a collectivity of voices: female and male, young and old, at various points on the political spectrum. An important aspect of Collins's revolutionary agenda is her transcription of the Creole language, and although she is hardly the first West Indian writer to attempt this, the combination of Creole with the multi-voiced, trans-generational narrative results in a novel so intensely lyrical that it could be called an extended prose poem.

The subject of *Angel* is revolutionary Grenada; however, to view the novel as "a call to arms," suggests propagandist service to one side in a binary opposition. Although Angel and other Grenadians take arms against the invading U.S forces, this is just a sideshow in a decades-long internal struggle for power. When the novel opens, Angel is an infant in her mother Doodsie's arms. Doodsie and her neighbors watch in silence as DeLisle plantation houses go up in flames. In a letter to a close female friend, Doodsie tells Ezra that "the country need a shake up like this," but she questions the integrity and methods of Leader (modeled on Eric Gairy) and deplores the confusion and violence plaguing the island nation: "I know we need a change but not in this way" (6-7). After Leader is released from jail, his rise to power encourages some members of the black population of Grenada, including Angel's father, Allan, who writes to his friend Martin: "You should see him, black as me you know and talking big with the best of the land" (44). By the end of the novel, however, when Angel is a young woman recently returned from studies at the University of the West Indies in Jamaica, the people are again taking to the streets in anger and violence to protest Leader's corrupt, self-serving government. His rival, referred to as Chief (Maurice Bishop), embodies the hopes of Angel's generation, but once again her mother Doodsie is skeptical, sensing that the secret Party of which Angel is a member is out of touch with the people and that the Revolution, which could only have succeeded with the people's support, is indifferent to its grass roots: "Dey not suppose to hide ting from us. Dey on top but is we dat make Revolution" (258). There is even dissention among members of the same generation. Angels' brother Rupert quarrels with his lover and his best friend because they think Chief is dishonest and arrogant. Angel resists Rupert's call for civil war, telling him that "we could solve nothing by going out there and shooting up each other!" Rupert responds by cursing the Party and turning his back on his older sister: "I not lyin, Angel. Ah disappointed. I always use to feel I learnin from you. All of a sudden is like wasn you talking" (270). Chief is killed, and the American invasion polarizes the generations. Doodsie, her husband Allan and her sister Jessie thank God for the intervention because it is the only way they see out of the chaos, while Angel argues that the U.S. is just trying to control the small country: "We wrong. We do real stupidness. But nobody don have a right to invade. We doesn invade dem when dey killin black people in their country" (274).

Angel loses an eye fighting the Americans, and ironically she must go to the U.S for treatment. Back in Grenada, she notices that the Delicia estate is being cut up and sold in small lots to the former workers, including her father. "Delicia estate was no more. And spirits don like to live same place wid people, said Doodsie. Jus now, you go see! Delicia gon lose its reputation for spirits!" (290). Angel holds a private wake for the restless spirits of her ancestors who were brought in shackles from Africa to labor on Delicia estate, and she lives up to her name by lighting candles to guide them into the next world: "They were either gone, or they sympathetic. Nothing to fraid" (291). By taking an active role in the welfare of her country, by suffering and risking death to defend Grenada against the American invaders, Angel comes to terms with the colonial history of the Caribbean and achieves parity with her ancestors whose blood and tears saturate the land that the people hope, at long last, to call their own.

Blood and land are recurring motifs in Collins's second novel, *The Colour of Forgetting*, beginning with the madwoman Carib's enigmatic chant, predicting doom: "Blood in the north, blood to come in the south, and the blue crying red in between" (3). Carib is the last in a line of women with the gift of prophecy, extending back to her great-grandmother, all with the same name. For four generations they have wandered the island of Paz, warning of blood, land confusion, warring factions, and the blue crying red in between.[6] When Willive Janvier goes to Carib for advice regarding her son William, nicknamed Thunder because of his profound fear of electrical storms, Carib responds: "Sometimes the children who should know most is the ones that know the least. Walk back. Walk back over all the story with him. Is the younger ones to stop the blue from crying red in between, but them self looking outside. They not listening inside here self. It is not that he don't know, but his head will get twist with all kind of other things he reading. He go be all right in the end, though. . . . Walk back with him. Walk back" (13-14).

The story that Willive has been charged with passing on to her son is the history of the Malheureuse family. Generations ago, during the time of slavery, a boss-man named Malheureuse murdered a slave named John Bull. "Time come and pass. Time bring a boss-man Malheureuse to a Great House. The Malheureuse blood pass on to the slave women generation that Boss-man Malheureuse breed. To John Bull nation. Mixture in the blood of the story. After a while people walking in the cane can't tell the difference between some of Malheureuse generation and John Bull nation" (18). One of the descendents of Malheureuse and John Bull, named Jim-Bull Malheureuse, produced Oldman who with his wife Magdalene produced six children: Caiphas, Isidora, Mayum, Adolphus, Son-Son, and Mamag. The bad blood finally manifests in Son-Son and his nephew Dolphus, who proceed to grab all the land from Dolphus's cousins who were not born in wedlock. Mamag outsmarts her brother and nephew by selling her family plot and buying a separate piece of land where she raises her five daughters. But Mayem's sons Ti-Moun and Cosmos are disinherited. Ti-Moun and his wife Cassandra, who is a direct descendent of John Bull, have only one child, Willive, before Ti-Moun is left brain damaged when he is at-tacked trying to defend his plot of land. Cassandra withdraws behind a wall of silence, and Willive is raised primarily by her great-aunt Mamag. Thunder, then is the most recent generation to be cursed by the unlucky Malheureuse blood, and Carib's advice to Willive—"Walk back over the all of the story with him"—suggests that the key to redemption is knowledge of the past.

Storytelling is an art passed down from Mamag to Willive and from Willive to Thunder. Thunder's father Ned, a reticent man, gradually opens up and also shares his family story with his son. Ned is named after one of his ancestors who, like John Bull, was murdered by a white man who was never brought to justice. Ned exhorts Thunder, when the latter is approaching manhood, not to forget his people once he has acquired an education: "What I telling you is, Ned couldn't talk for himself those times. And nobody of our people, the black peo-ple, the African people who they call slaves like Ned and so, couldn't do a thing to help him. So now is the generations to come, like you and everybody who getting an education, have to write Ned name in the ground, have to say all the things that Ned couldn't say" (141). However, as Carib had predicted when Thunder was just a small boy, his head has gotten "twist with all kind of other things he reading" (13). When Thunder returns from England with his degree in accountancy, his radical ideas about land ownership alienate him from his par-ents, who have an opportunity to buy back some of the land that was stolen by Willive's uncle and cousin. "So we, how all-you does say the word, we petty-bourgeois, right?" Ned asks his son in anger. "I talk to you since you in school about letting friend experience go with you head. Other people life is not yours. Land! You whole family history tell you what land mean and instead of explain-ing to friend, you sit down there listening to what friend say. . . . What they know about land? You self you don't know nothing, but you family live it. So you know!" (156-7).

Land confusion, mixture in the blood, "and the blue crying red in between." Another generation torn by land disputes and the Malheureuse curse. Carib's prophesy comes true when blood is shed in Paz during riots and revolution in 1979, and although his parents achieve their goal of purchasing land, Thunder himself fails to fulfill the promise that Carib hoped for in his generation. He quits his job, moves up into the hills, and neglects the daughter he fathered years ago, before he left for England. "You is me son," Willive tells him, "but honest to goodness it sicken me to see how all-you man could ignore you children, not to talk about yourself. . . . She, the mother, she didn't have no choice. Is why all-you could talk so much about life, because you don't know not one damn thing about it. Sounding jefe and somebody else doing all the work!" (200). Although still a young man, Thunder seems to have given up. He tells his father that his daughter Nehanda is his only hope: "I up there by the lake worrying about the past, but Nehanda, she in front. I don't know if you know what I saying, but the way how I feel is Nehanda generation, yes, that will write the names that we ignore all this time. Is Nehanda generation" (210).

As Thunder passes the torch to the next generation, Carib continues to preach: "Blood in the north, blood in the south, and is the children to stop the blue from crying red in between. . . . But is the children to know and to stop it" (212). Blue is "the colour for forgetting" (207), and the children must write the names, keep the past alive, so that future generations will not make the same mistakes and suffer over land disputes and mixture in the blood. But in the final scene, as Carib returns by sea to Paz from the neighboring island of Eden, the boat passes over an under-water volcano and the turbulence causes a child to choke to death on its own vomit. The infant's death bodes ill for a nation waiting for "the children to stop the blue from crying red in between."

Collins takes the novel of development to a new level by making relational autonomy not only a measure of maturity, but also the structuring principle of the novels themselves in which dialogue across generational, gender and political lines subverts the traditional perception in character as an individual and autonomous self. The true protagonist in *Angel* and especially *The Colour of Forgetting* is the community and the nation as a whole, including long-dead ancestors and generations to come, the nation's hope for the future.[7]

In the novels of Collins, Cliff, Edgell, Kincaid and many other contemporary West Indian women writers, Bakhtin's vision of the novel's potential is fulfilled with "the historical emergence of the world itself," a world struggling to break free of its colonial past while maintaining a vital link to that past in the form of stories that "talk for" the voiceless, powerless members of previous generations. When emerging nations establish that precarious balance being "apart from" while still "a part of" their painful histories, they move toward relational autonomy, which can be viewed as a measure of their vitality and durability.

Notes

1. According to Jeffrey L. Sammons, "the concept of *Bildung* is intensely bourgeois; it carries with it many assumptions about the autonomy and relative integrity of the self," assumptions that have become increasingly difficult to sustain the modern world (42). As the term *Bildungsroman* loses touch with its bourgeois humanistic roots and is applied to novels with radically different historical and ideological parameters, Sammons argues, it becomes less useful as a tool in genre studies.
2. Fraiman worries that "those theories of female developmental fiction that recuperate a wholly different plot of spiritual growth and domestic relationships" will continue to marginalize women by remaining "too obligingly within the given contours of 'women's culture,' neglecting the troubling appeal and predominance of the *Bildungsroman* for female figures" (143-4). Fraiman is uncomfortable with the *Bildungsroman's* idealization of Romantic individualism, and she suggests that female coming-of-age narratives by nineteenth-century English writers should be read "less as a wholly alternative structure than as an ironization and interrogation of the old" (126-7).
3. I have discussed the first stage of relational autonomy in "Dialogic Interplay in Coming-of-Age Novels by West Indian Women Writers."

4. See Ronnie Natov for a discussion of the adolescent girl's "regressive long-ing" for an "original pre-oedipal state of merging with the mother," which is in conflict with an equal and opposite need "to separate from the mother," a sepa-ration that entails a partial denial of the self (2).

5. Because Mariah is a wealthy, white American, while Lucy is poor and black, and from a developing nation, this oppressive mother-daughter relationship ac-crues political significance, with Mariah representing the U.S. interests, and Lucy the insufficiently grateful small island nation beholden to the superpower.

6. Carib is "mad" in the sense that Foucault describes the pre-Renaissance view of mental illness as "a dramatic debate in which [man] confronted the secret powers of the world; the experience of madness was clouded by images of the Fall and the Will of God, of the Beast and the Metamorphosis, and of all the marvelous secrets of Knowledge" (xii).

7. Collins is writing in a tradition of Caribbean literature initiated in the 1950s by George Lamming. In his 1983 Introduction to *In the Castle of My Skin* (1953), Lamming explains that the shift in focus from the individual to the community, in his novels and those of other Caribbean writers, "has caused some difficulty for the conventional critic of the novel." Lamming explains that his novel "is crowded with names and people, and although each character is accorded a most vivid presence and force of personality, we are rarely con-cerned with the prolonged exploration of the individual consciousness. It is the collective human substance of the Village itself which commands our attention. The Village, you might say, is the central character" (xxxvi).

Works Cited

Bakhtin, Mikhail M. "The *Bildungsroman* and Its Significance in the History of Realism (Toward a Historical Typology of the Novel)." *Speech Genres and Other Late Essays*. University of Texas Press Slavic Series 8. Trans. Vern W. McGee. Ed. Caryl Emerson and Michael Holquist. 1986. Austin: Uni-versity of Texas Press, 1992.

Burton, Stacy. "Bakhtin, Temporality, and Modern Narrative: Writing 'the Whole Triumphant Murderous Unstoppable Chute.'" *Comparative Litera-ture* 48.1 (1996): 39-64

Cliff, Michelle. *Abeng*. 1984. New York: Penguin, 1991.

———. "Adrift in Female Terrain." *Ms.* July/August 1993: 76-78.

———. *No Telephone to Heaven*, 1987. New York: Vintage, 1989.

Collins, Merle. *Angel*. London: The Women's Press, 1987.

———. *The Colour of Forgetting*. London: Virago, 1995.

Edgell, Zee. *Beka Lamb*. 1982. London: Heinemann, 1986.

———. *In Times Like These*. London: Heinemann, 1991.

Edmondson, Belinda. "Race, Privilege, and the Politics of (Re)writing History: An Analysis of the Novels of Michelle Cliff." *Callaloo* 16.1 (1993): 180-191.

Foucault, Michel. *Madness and Civilization: A History of Insanity in the Age of Reason*. Trans. Richard Howard. 1961. New York: Vintage, 1982.

Fraiman, Susan. *Unbecoming Women: British Women Writers and the Novel of Development.* New York: Columbia University Press, 1993.

Holquist, Michael. *Bakhtin and his World.* New York: Routledge, 1990.

Keller, Evelyn Fox. *Reflections on Gender and Science.* New Haven, Yale University Press, 1985.

Kincaid, Jamaica. *Annie John.* 1983, New York: NAL/Plume, 1985.

————. *Lucy.* New York: Plume, 1991.

Lamming, George. Introduction (1983). 1953. *In the Castle of My Skin.* Ann Arbor: University of Michigan Press, 1991.

Lima, Maria Helena. "Revolutionary Developments: Michelle Cliff's *No Telephone to Heaven* and Merle Collins's *Angel*." *ARIEL* 24.1 (1993): 35-56.

Moses, Michael Valdez. "Caliban and His Precursors: The Politics of Literary History and the Third World." *Theoretical Issues in Literary History.* Harvard English Studies 16. Ed. David Perkins. Cambridge: Harvard University Press, 1991.

Natov, Roni. "Mothers and Daughters: Jamaica Kincaid's Pre-Oedipal Narrative." *Children's Literature* 18 (1990): 1-16.

Sammons, Jeffrey L. "The Bildungsroman for Nonspecialists: An Attempt at Clarification." *Reflection And Action: Essays on the Bildungsroman.* Ed. James Hardin. Columbia, SC: University of South Carolina Press, 1991.

Schultz, Karen. "Women's Adult Development: The Importance of Friendship." *Journal of Independent Social Work* 5.2 (1991): 19-30.

Wilson, Lucy. "Dialogic Interplay in Coming-of-Age Novels by West Indian Women Writers." *Children's Literature Association Quarterly* 18.4 (1993-94): 176-182.

Aging and Ageism in Paule Marshall's *Praisesong for the Widow* and Beryl Gilroy's *Frangipani House*

Typically we think of exile as a fundamental dislocation brought about by distance from one's home and roots, intensified by race, religion, ethnic origins, class, as well as gender. Another kind of exile, however, is the separation and alienation that results from the inevitable and inexorable process of aging. It is exemplified by a character like Beryl Gilroy's Mama King, who has lived her entire life in one place.

Herbert Blau observes "the unreconciled children" growing impatient with the "almost obscene ubiquity" of the elderly. "So we consign them," he continues, "with mixed feelings to a sort of exiled behavior which, as the children themselves join the multitudes of age, they may later come to regret" (21). Along similar lines but focusing exclusively on ageism as it affects women, Baba Cooper writes that the ageism experienced by old women "is firmly embedded in sexism—an extension of the male power to define, control values, erase, disempower and divide. Woman to woman ageism is an aspect of the horizontal conflict that usurps the energies of the colonized—part of the female competition for the crumbs of social power" (73). The elderly, the elderly women in particular, are exiles, cut off from the sources of power and pleasure in a world that worships firm bodies and smooth skin, a materialistic world that places higher value on physical appearance than it does on mental and spiritual attributes.

Despite the universality of aging, relatively little has been written about women and aging, either in fiction or criticism.[1] For men it is another story. Blau notes the presence of "something in the disposition of the major modernists—Stevens, James, Proust, Mann, Joyce, Eliot, Marx, and Freud—that has an affinity with age and aging. . . . It is a disadvantaged history, of course, the history of the modern, because it is a history dominated and written by men" (24). Women writers since Woolf have begun to tilt the balance of this male-dominated history. Among others, Paule Marshall and Beryl Gilroy not only depict the pain, isolation, suffering and indignities that so often accompany old age, but also suggest the untapped potential of older women as a source of wisdom, insight and self-esteem for younger generations.

In her study of contemporary women poets who have written about aging, Diana Hume George admits that, initially, she wished that the poets would teach her how to grow old, would endow her with a wisdom and grant her the blessing that "would correspond to Erickson's eighth stage of psycho-social developments, that tidy place called 'integrity'" (134-36). Instead, what she found was the "crystallization, the intensely crowded concentration of attention, of the mind upon its sources and origins" in a personal, psychoanalytic, Oedipal, and even pre-Oedipal context (136). In my study of Paule Marshall's *Praisesong for the Widow* and Gilroy's *Frangipani House*, I also found a return of the mind to its sources—personal as well as racial, ethnic and historical. This return was accomplished by means of metaphor, especially the metaphorical journey, and by the structural or thematic juxtaposition of different periods of time. While the protagonists in these two novels achieve a state similar to Erickson's eighth stage of psycho-social development, there are some significant departures from Erickson's model, but particularly in *Frangipani House*. Nonetheless, both writers communicate a special kind of wisdom, an awareness that "symbolic action perpetuates our lives" (Schwartz 6), and this awareness manifests itself in terms of ritual.[2]

Deborah E. McDowell maintains that the motif of the journey in the novels of black women writers "is basically a personal and psychological journey" (194-95). This is no doubt true of Avey Johnson's journey in *Praisesong for the Widow*. From her comfortable home in North White Plains, New York, to the tiny island of Carriacou, off the coast of Grenada, her voyage has social as well as political implications, for Avey and her late husband Jerome (Jay) Johnson, in their struggle to achieve the "American Dream," had lost touch with what was most important. They abandoned their private, intimate rituals, and only at the age of sixty-four does Avey being to realize that "something in those small rites, an ethos they had in common, had reached back beyond her life and beyond Jay's to join them to a vast unknown lineage that had made their being possible . . . had both protected them and put them in possession of a kind of power" (137). Avey questions the nature of the Faustian bargain that they struck. "How much had they foolishly handed over in exchange for the things they had gained?" (139-40). The answers are revealed by the many flashbacks to the time when Jerome Johnson was still alive, speaking disparagingly of less fortunate black men and women "in the harsh voice that treated them as a race apart." Although Avey would sometimes object, she too "lived through most of the sixties and early seventies as if Watts and Selma and the tanks and Stoner guns in the streets of Detroit somehow did not pertain to her, denying her rage, and carefully effacing any dream that might have come to her during the night by the time she awoke the next morning" (140).

Avey not only denies her heritage by living in affluent North *White* Plains and vacationing on the cruise ship *Bianca Pride*, but also she spends the greater part of her life refusing the mission which her great-aunt Cuney had entrusted her while Avey was still a child; "a mission she couldn't even name yet had felt duty-bound to fulfill" until she was able "to rid herself of the notion" (42). This mission, she knew even as a little girl, was somehow connected to the story of the Ibos, "those pure-born Africans," who "could see in more ways than one" (37). When the Ibos arrived by boat on Tatem Island on the South Carolina Tidewater, they took a "long hard look" at the unfamiliar landscape and at the white people who had brought them to this place, a look that included the history of the black race in the New World right up to the present day. Then they turned around and walked across the ocean "like the water was solid ground," singing as they returned to their home in Africa. Aunt Cuney's grandmother witnessed this event and passed the story down. Avey, named "Avatara" after that same ancestor, thought that she could escape the burden of history. However, one night on the *Bianca Pride*, she dreams, much to her horror, that she is engaged in a physical struggle with her long-dead great-aunt, in front of her white neighbors in North White Plains, which signals the return of these and other long-suppressed memories to her conscious mind.

Hoping to catch a plane to New York that same day, Avey abandons her friends and the cruise ship at Grenada. But events conspire to keep her on the island where, after another uneasy night, this time reliving in detail the decay of her marriage and the metamorphosis of her loving husband "Jay" into the joyless Jerome Johnson, Avey meets Lebert Joseph. A wily trickster, he convinces her to make the Carriacou Excursion. Velma Pollard has compared Lebert Joseph to the Voodoo god Legba, who usually "presents himself as an old, lame man" (289). This makes the ageless, androgynous Lebert Joseph a most appropriate leader of a ceremony that, according to Barbara Christian, "combines rituals from several black societies; the Ring Dances of Tatum, Bojangles of New York, the Voodoo drums of Haiti, [and] the rhythms of the various African peoples brought to the New World" (82).

The dance is just one of the devices Marshall uses to collapse personal and historical time into ritual timelessness. The boat trip from Grenada to Carriacou on the *Emanuel C*, for example, recalls to Avey's mind boat rides up the Hudson on the *Robert Fulton* when she was a girl. At those times she felt a mystical connection with the other passengers, as though silken threads issued out of their navels and hearts, threads that felt "as strong entering her as the lifelines of woven hemp that trailed out into the water at Coney Island" (191). On the *Emanuel C*, Avey is helped and comforted during a violent and embarrassing attack of seasickness by several very old women who remind her of "the presiding mothers of Mount Olivet Baptist [her own mother's church long ago] . . . all those whose great age and long service to the church had earned them a title even more distinguished than 'sister' and a place of honor in the pews up front" (194). The narrator observes that these old people "have the essentials to go on forever," advancing a theme set in motion by the first appearance of Lebert Joseph, which reaches its fullest expression during the following night's ceremony on Carriacou.

The Carriacou Excursion is an annual event which draws together everyone from the island, young and old, even though many have made homes for themselves on Grenada. They gather to honor the Old Parents, to sing the Big Pardon, and to perform the nation dances. Significantly, only the old people are allowed to dance the Temne, Banda, Moko, Cromanti, Congo and Chamba nation dances; the old in this community hold a position of power and privilege. Later in the evening, the younger people join in the Creole dances, but even during the energetic jump-up, the old people on the perimeter dance "the rhythmic trudge that couldn't be called dancing, yet at the same time was something more than merely walking. A non-dance designed to conserve their failing strength and see them through the night" (246). Avey rejects the false values that she had adopted during her marriage when she joins in "the restrained glide-and-stamp, the rhythmic trudge, the Carriacou Tramp, the shuffle designed to stay the course of history" (250). The other dancers, in reverent acknowledgement of the transformation that has occurred in her, turn and bow to Avey, Avatara—she to whom the sacred trust of the Ibos has been handed down through the generations.

From this rich evocation of the vast spiritual and historical significance of old age and ancestry, we turn to a far bleaker portrait of an older and much poorer woman in *Frangipani House*, Beryl Gilroy's novel, named for the expensive nursing home to which Mrs. Mabel Alexandria King, Mama King, has been committed by her well-meaning daughters. Like Lebert Joseph, who mourns his "grands and great-grands born in that place [he] has never seen" (Marshall 168), Mama King lives far from her children and American-born grandchildren. And like Jerome Johnson, Mama King's daughters have assumed the values of their adopted country and the white race. They agree to pay five-hundred dollars a month to have "white people care for her" (Gilroy 3), and they mistakenly assume that because the rest home is costly, their mother is content to live there.

Nothing, however, could be further from the truth. Life at Frangipani House has systematically robbed Mama King of everything that gave her life meaning. In *Vital Involvement in Old Age*, Erik Erickson, Joan Erickson, and Helen Kivnick discuss the difficulty some elderly people experience as a result of mandatory retirement: "for those whose creativity and involvement in work has been of major importance and whose identity is largely derived from that work, there can be a bitter and deprived feeling of being expelled and depreciated" (299). This is certainly true of Mama King, whom a nurse scolds saying she is lucky because "life is a treadmill. You been on it for years and years. You daughters push you off. Don't grumble. Don't complain. Count your blessings" (16). But Mama King will not be placated. "More than anything else she wanted to work. Her body needed it as it needed food and clothes. And now, time and life, her daughters and the matron had all conspired to deprive her of her faithful friends, work and hardship" (19). The "treadmill" of hard work that Nurse Douglas spoke of so disparagingly was the source of the old woman's pride and strength:

> Mama King thought of all the distance she had walked in the life, all the loads of wood and bags of charcoal, buckets of water, trays of washing and heavy fruit she had carried on her single, strong head, which in spite of everything had kept its shape. Feeling her head as if to reassure herself that it had not been changed in any way by over-use and years of faithful service, she marveled at its strength. (24)

But work is not the only thing Mama King misses. During a rainstorm, Mama King identifies with "a picture card at the mercy of the rushing water," with "no control over its route or its fate" (31). When an old acquaintance, Ben Le Cage, visits her, he asks, "Why do they do this to her? As long as she lives, she has to be active. Sitting around made her mad" (34). Miss Ginchi, Mama King's friend since childhood, comes to the same conclusion: "Confinement and do-nothing destroy people. She like to hustle. She hustle all her life" (48). When one of Mama King's grandchildren, Markey, flies in from his naval base in the Caribbean, he is appalled by the change in her:

He remembered her dark-haired and strong, able to get the stopper from a bottle with her teeth. She was purposeful and positive. Now here she was, a haunted ghost with a haunting past. The family had imagined her happy, interminably giving and caring and sharing in friendship and community. Never getting older. Immortal. What had the years done to her? True, she had been ill. But this was more than illness. She was old, but age did not enhance or dignify her. What had they done to her? (46-47)

What "they" had done to Mama King was to deprive her of work, control, action, community, hardship, and self-actualization.

In the study cited above, many of the elderly subjects "speak of the importance to them of the independent living they have known and of their real horror of 'those homes for the elderly.' They feel supported by their familiar settings, by the neighborhood in which they have lived and are known" (310). The authors state that:

> Unfortunately, these homes for the aged are too often run solely as business ventures, and expenditures are minimized for the sake of profit. It is in many ways less costly and more practical to take care of patients on a routine schedule than to allow for individual differences in capacities and needs. The operating of institutions in such mechanical ways degrades both the staff and the patients, since it fails to acknowledge and accommodate the strengths and needs of the individual. (314-15)

This description fits Frangipani House and its staff. "In a show of power," Nurse Agnes pulls a pillow from beneath the head of a sleeping Mama King (26). In another incident, Matron Trask, "fed up" with Mama King's crying and disoriented ramblings, forces her to remove her false teeth and eat two big sausages, "but the thick rubbery skin defie[s] her gums" (35). Even the patients in the nursing home are capable of cruelty toward one another, as when Miss Turvey taunts Mama King: "The bus break down! The wheel come off! The driver dead! You grandson ain' comin! Ha ha-ha-ha-ha-ha-ha!" (45).

When Mama King escapes from Frangipani House with a band of beggars, and roams with them for several weeks, she eats less well but feels stronger and happier than she has in a long time. Pandit, Sumintra and the other beggars restore to Mama King her sense of self-worth, and gradually her mind clears as she performs again the daily tasks necessary for survival. But Mama King loses her freedom, and nearly her life, when she is attacked by a gang of youths in the fish market. Her disappearance and her subsequent return to Frangipani House, close to death, bring her daughters and grandchildren back to Guyana, but the scene that unfolds, once Mama King is on the mend, is both sad and farcical. Cyclette, the younger daughter, pays lip service to the idea of bringing Mama King home with her, but "Aunty Cyclette is all mouth," her nephew Solomon warns (96). Solo himself is about to be married and is too full of dreams about his future as an eye doctor to have time for his ailing grandmother. Markey is committed to the navy, and Mama King's older daughter, Token, makes no pretense about the matter:

I'm going back to where *I* am—to where the life that is mine exists. This place is the past—the painful past. Mama never wanted more than this. This is her life, not mine. I never wanted to be like her—her altruism sickened me. Her patience—her low, low goals. Just look at her. Worn out—worked out for nothing. (98)

Cyclette sobs, "There is nothing here for me either . . . Just pain and hatred of poverty, hardship and useless mud and dung, pain, mosquitoes and old age." Markey cries too, calling Mama King "just a heap of old age," and admitting that it is "hard associating with poverty to this degree."

Mama King raised both her daughters and all her grandchildren, yet only Cindy, the grandchild who was so difficult that she and Solomon were sent to the States, is eager to rescue the old woman from the nursing home. Cindy, whose pregnancy is at an advanced stage, is infuriated that her baby is "coming into a family that look upon great-grandmother as a burden" (94). Cindy's husband, Chuck, who has lived for a year in Africa, rejects what he calls "Caucasian solutions" and insists that they "have to go back to the African village for answers. The old in Africa have a place and a function. They are never cast aside" (95). Later, Chuck questions his somewhat facile assumptions about African life, but he feels strongly as Cindy does that Mama King belongs with them.

Mama King has other plans, however. She wants to return to Pandit's band of beggars, and she insists that "the only real kindness I ever get was from beggars. . . . They give me back my senses because they treat me like I was somebody" (94). She enjoyed that life because it was risky, "like going to catch fish at high tide on rough water" (96). When the police warn the beggars to leave her alone, Mama King tells Cindy and Chuck, "I know where I want to go. But I can't. I will have to go with you two" (101). Mama King's desire to rejoin the beggars might seem foolish, and her grudging acceptance of Cindy and Chuck's offer may appear ungrateful, but this, in fact, reveals Mama King as a complex character. Despite the Ericksons' view of grandparenting as "the culmination of the parenting role" and "one of the most positive and vital involvements of old age" (*Vital Involvement* 306), not all elderly persons are content with the "*grand*-generative function" of Erickson's eighth stage of psycho-social development (*Life Cycle* 63). Mama King's love for Token and Cyclette's offspring is apparent in the many flashbacks to their childhood years, but she also feels a long-suppressed rage when she thinks: "*They never ask me if I want to be mother and father again and again. Nobody ever ask me! They just make it so I got to do it*" (20). Mama King does agree to live with Cindy and Chuck, but not without further misgivings. After Cindy's twins are born, Mama King says, "You're a family now. You have everything . . . you don't need me. I stayin' here in this house my brother Abel buy for me" (109). Like her mother and aunt before her, Cindy begs Mama King to help her raise the twins, and the old woman consents, but with a strong warning: "'I will do the best I can,' she said. 'But,' she added fiercely, 'my heart brittle—like an eggshell. It easy to break'" (109).

Baba Copper, herself a grandmother who has chosen a non-traditional lifestyle to the dismay of her daughters, reflects on the assumption—held in Nicaragua, the Soviet Union, China and the United States—that a grandmother's main function is to provide alternative child care when their daughters go to work:

> First the men unload responsibility for their children upon women, then women become liberated and unload their children on their old mothers. . . . Liberation for women means old women too. I know that these grandmothers are often the ones who insist that . . . grandchildren give them a reason for living. I also recognize that the old women in the United States often unwillingly live far away from their grandchildren. None of this legitimizes exploiting old women in unpaid jobs which repeat the stresses of their child rearing years. Service is not necessarily the *function* of age in women. (9)

By resisting the grand-generative function and fighting for freedom and independence, Mama King challenges the stereotypes associated with old age. Instead of sitting back and "acting her age," she continues to let life "reconstitute" her—"first as a child, then as a woman, wife, mother, grandmother, mad-head old woman, beggar, and finally old woman at peace at last" (Gilroy 104).

On the surface, *Frangipani House* and *Prasiesong for the Widow* end similarly, with the protagonists headed to the United States, after a symbolic journey (Avey's trip to Carriacau and Mama King's four weeks of wandering) and a rediscovery of each woman's identity. However, there are some marked differences. Marshall's Avey Johnson achieves a profound sense of identity by connecting with her African heritage, but the novel ends abruptly with Avey on her way back home with a grandiose scheme to haunt the streets and lawns of North White Plains, the mall and train station, and the office buildings in downtown Manhattan. "Like the obsessed old sailor she had read about in high school," she would accost the brightest and best of the younger generation, "and before they could pull out of her grasp, tell them about the floor in Halsey Street and quote them the line from her namesake" (255). She also plans to rebuild the house which her great-aunt had left her in Tatum, and to demand that her grandchildren spend their summers there learning about the Ibos, as she had been given the account by Aunt Cuney. This is all very impressive but unconvincing, since her euphoria is the heady stuff of New Year's resolutions and has not stood the test of time.

On the other hand, Gilroy's Mama King continues to experience life on a day-to-day, even minute-by-minute basis; her rituals are the daily, intimate motions of life, which she shares with her granddaughter: "The women from the lane often stopped for 'women-talk and time-waste,' which meant discussing their own childbirth experiences" (105). Cindy thanks Mama King and the other women for their strength and support, adding that "Chuck sure will get the same support from your men. Sure thing." The women respond: "Support! They wouldn't give him support. They will give him rum—white rum, bush rum and five year rum. Shoor ting" (106). Though lacking the rhetorical intensity of Marshall's novel, Gilroy's *Frangipani House* captures the lyrical rhythms of tropical life and language.

Both Avey Johnson and Mama King rise Phoenix-like from the ashes of their past lives to face new challenges in their remaining years. Each woman achieves a renewed sense of self worth after a shattering encounter with mortality: Avey's illness and fear of drowning on the boat to Carriacau, and Mama King's near-fatal beating in the fish market. In a sense, these elderly women have turned the exile of old age into a metaphor for the human condition, since ultimately we must all relinquish our hold on the familiar and embrace non-being:

> At the extremities of existence, the entire structuring process may be called into question, as the achievements of selfhood are confronted inevitably by another paradox, the presence of non-being. Can we mourn the loss of *ourselves*? The ultimate paradox may be that the knowable reality of the self is its *symbolic* status, beyond which nothing is thinkable. (Schwartz 5)

This insight into the symbolic nature of selfhood infuses the work of Marshall and Gilroy with great power. It accounts for the importance of ritual—the nation dances and Beg Pardon, the "woman-talk" and "waste-time"—in both novels. Finally, this is the *raison d'être* for the pervasiveness of the journey motif, since all voyages and journeys presage a final dislocation into ultimate exile.

Notes

1. Although not strictly literary in their focus, in addition to Baba Copper's book, there are several works that deal with women and aging. Simone de Beauvoir recalls her mother's last days in *A Very Easy Death*, translated by Patrick O'Brian (New York: Pantheon Books, 1965). Susan Hemmings has collected essays by eighteen women between the ages of forty and sixty-five in *A Wealth of Experience: The Lives of Older Women* (London: Pandora Press, 1985). Barbara G. Walker's *The Crone: Women of Age, Wisdom, and Power* (San Francisco: Harper & Row, 1985) examines the need for a rediscovery of the crone archetype, which has been systematically subverted by patriarchal institutions.
2. In *The Life Cycle Completed*, Erickson summarizes the chief characteristics of his eight stages of psychosocial development and describes "the dominant syntonic trait in the last stage" as *integrity*, which he defines as "a comradeship with the ordering ways of distant times and different pursuits, as expressed in their simple products and sayings" (64-65). He claims that "a historical change like the lengthening of the average life span calls for viable reritualizations, which must provide a meaningful interplay between beginning and end as well as some finite sense of summary and, possibly, a more active anticipation of dying" (63). These reritualizations comprise *wisdom*, which he presents as an antidote to *despair* in old age. Diana Hume George's skepticism with regard to the "tidiness" of Erickson's scheme is echoed by Simone de Beauvoir in the work cited above, when she maintains that "[t]here is no such thing as a natural death" since death is always "an unjustifiable violation" (106). Joseph T. Skerrett has compared Paule Marshall's three major characters to Erickson's scheme. But Skerrett fo-

cuses on Merle Kinbona and does not explore the implications of Avery Johnson's "crisis of integrity" ["Paule Marshall and the Crisis of Middle Years: *The Chosen Place, The Timeless People.*" *Callaloo* 6.2 (1983): 68-73].

Works Cited

Blau, Herbert. "The Makeup of Memory in the Winter of Our Discontent." Woodward and Schwartz 13-36.

Christian, Barbara T. "Ritualistic Process and the Structure of Palue Marshall's *Praisesong for the Widow.*" *Callaloo* 6.2 (Spring-Summer 1983): 74-84.

Copper, Baba. *Over the Hill: Reflections on Ageism Between Women.* Freedom, California: The Crossing Press, 1988.

Erikson, Erik H. *The Life Cycle Completed: A Review.* 1982. New York: W.W. Norton & Company, 1985.

Erikson, Erik H., Joan M. Erikson, and Helen Q. Kivnick. *Vital Involvement in Old Age.* New York: W.W. Norton & Company, 1986.

George, Diana Hume. "'Who Is the Double Ghost Whose Head Is Smoke?' Women Poets on Aging." Woodward and Schwartz 134-53.

Gilroy, Beryl. *Frangipani House.* London: Heinemann Educational Books, Ltd., 1986.

Marshall, Paule. *Praisesong for the Widow.* London: Virago Press, 1983.

McDowell, Deborah E. "New Directions for Black Feminist Criticism." *The New Feminist Criticism: Essays on Women, Literature, and Theory.* Ed. Elaine Showalter. New York: Pantheon Books, 1985. 186-99.

Pollard, Velma. "Cultural Connections in Paule Marshall's *Praisesong for the Widow.*" *World Literature Written in English* 25.2 (Autumn 1985): 285-98.

Schwartz, Murray M. "Introduction." Woodward and Schwartz 1-12.

Woodward, Kathleen and Murray M. Schwartz, eds. *Memory and Desire: Aging—Literature—Psychoanalysis.* Bloomington: Indiana University Press, 1986.

Reading Kincaid's *The Autobiography of My Mother*

The Autobiography of My Mother marks a significant departure from Jamaica Kincaid's earlier novels, *Annie John* and *Lucy*, in that the narrator of Kincaid's third novel is a woman in her seventies, although we do not learn this until six pages from the end.[1] As she relates the events of her life, Xuela Claudette Richardson speaks in many voices: an abandoned, motherless child; an adolescent coerced prematurely into sexual activity; a reclusive young woman attempting to rebuild her life after a near-fatal abortion; a woman with great physical needs who fears exposing her vulnerability; the daughter of a man incapable of love; the wife of a man she does not love; and finally, an old woman longing "to meet the thing greater than I am, the thing to which I can submit" (*Autobiography* 228). In *The Autobiography of My Mother*, Jamaica Kincaid avoids stereotypes of old age, both negative and positive. Xuela in her seventies is neither an ineffectual old woman nor a wise "crone" figure. She is what she has always been: a fiercely intelligent, angry, but ultimately accepting individual who glories in her role as "one of the vanquished" and turns defeat into victory and revenge.

Herbert Blau has observed that despite the preoccupation of the major modernists with age and aging, women's voices and experiences have constantly been underrepresented because "the history of the modern . . . is a history dominated and written by men" (24). Women writers, including Virginia Woolf, Jean Rhys, Paule Marshall, Beryl Gilroy and now Jamaica Kincaid, have begun to redress the injustice done to women in this male-dominated discussion of aging by using stories and novels to explore the consciousness of middle-aged and elderly female protagonists.[2] And the recent work of theorists such as Diana Hume George and Kathleen Woodward provides a critical and psychoanalytical context for the discussion of women, aging, and literature. In an essay on women poets and aging, George recalls her initial approach to her subjects as daughter and acolyte seeking wisdom and blessings. She had hoped to find that "these courageous women" had reached a point in their lives that "would correspond to Erik Erikson's eighth stage of psychosocial development, that tidy place called 'integrity'" (136). For Erikson and his co-authors, integrity offsets despair and hopelessness in old age by "integrating maturing forms of hope, will, purpose, competence, fidelity, love, and care into a comprehensive sense of wisdom" (Erikson, Erikson and Kivnick 55-56). However, George discovered that the writers she examined did not have all the answers, had not overcome their fear of aging and dying. George observes that "their poetry records the process rather than the final result . . . these poets *use* their fears in the continuing process of coming to terms with their aging, with their dying" (135).

Kathleen Woodward also expresses reservations about Erikson's romanticized "wise old man" or "wise old woman," and in place of "integrity," Woodward postulates "the mirror stage of old age" which is the inverse of Lacan's mirror stage of infancy:

> As in the mirror stage of infancy, in the mirror stage of old age the subject identifies with an image and in so doing is transformed. If in the case of the former the infant enters the imaginary, in the latter the subject enters the social realm reserved for senior citizens in the Western world. But the point is that the subject resists this identification rather than embraces it because what is whole is felt to reside *within* the subject and the image in the mirror is understood as uncannily prefiguring the disintegration and nursling dependence of advanced age. ("Mirror" 110)

Woodward suggests that it might be psychologically healthy "to reject one's image as old," although she acknowledges that such denial marginalizes the elderly and may in fact be counterproductive for writers since, as Proust observed toward the end of his life, "creativity and illness are often linked, and often indissolubly so" ("Mirror" 103).

Woodward advances her theories of aging and literature in "Late Theory, Late Style," noting that old age in our culture is usually associated with loneliness and loss. "But loss can continue to be transformative throughout old age as well as in other times of our lives. Grief can continue to be a force for change" ("Late Theory" 83). Woodward takes issue with Freud's theories in "Mourning and Melancholia," particularly his view that melancholia is pathological, while mourning is "normal." Woodward explains Freud's view of mourning as "psychic work which has a precise purpose and goal—to 'free' ourselves from the emotional bonds which have tied us to the person we loved so that we may 'invest' that energy elsewhere, to 'detach' ourselves so that we may be 'uninhibited'" (85). When the work of mourning is completed, when we have divested ourselves of pain and grief, mourning must come to an end. Melancholia, on the other hand, "is characterized primarily as a state, not a process. It is denial of the reality of loss. It is a 'disorder,' a 'disease.' Melancholia is ultimately failed, or unsuccessful, mourning" (85-86). Objecting to Freud's clinical tone and pious, "almost ethical injunction to kill the dead and to adjust ourselves to 'reality,'" Woodward argues that "Freud leaves us here with no room for another place, one between a crippling melancholia and the end of mourning" (86). She observes that Freud's own life and work defied this binary construction: he never "recovered" from the loss of his little grandson who died when Freud was sixty-seven, yet he went on to publish one of his most revolutionary works, *Inhibitions, Symptoms and Anxiety*, three years later.

Woodward contrasts Freud's "Mourning and Melancholia" with Roland Barthes's *Camera Lucida*, in which Barthes mourns his beloved mother:

> I read Barthes's self-portrait of his bereavement for his mother as a figure and performance of his interminable grief. For me this haunting text, defined as its contents and as a tangible object (the book itself), represents the possibility of a response to loss that situates itself between mourning and melancholia. The book itself embodies a resistance to mourning which entails a kind of willed refusal to relinquish pain. (89)

Just as Freud's irreconcilable loss of his grandson led to the production of a great late work, Barthes's pain and loss contributed to the creation of this extraordinary book: "Barthes insists in *Camera Lucida* that he could not '*transform*' his pain, but his pain radically transformed his style. . . . With *Camera Lucida* as our text we may conclude that the refusal to allow mourning to run its so-called normal course can vivify and not impoverish a life" (95). Woodward concludes that it may not always be possible or desirable to detach ourselves from pain and to forget our loss. (Woodward's own reading and writing about mourning began with a profound personal loss.) She observes that loss and pain can be a catalyst not only for writing but for action, as in the case of AIDS activist Douglas Crimp, whose grief and rage "have transformed mourning into militancy" (96). The experience of grief and rage as a catalyst for politicization and writing is critical to an understanding of the novels of Jamaica Kincaid.

When Jamaica Kincaid, in her mid-forties, decided to write a retrospective narrative from the point of view of a woman in her seventies, it was not the wise crone figure that she envisioned, nor was it a sweet grandmotherly type, despite Erikson's view of grandparenting as "the culmination of the parenting role" and "one of the most positive and vital involvements of old age" (306). From birth, Xuela's life was built on loss, grief and anger: "My mother died at the moment I was born, and so for my whole life there was nothing standing between myself and eternity; at my back was always a bleak, bleak wind. . . . I came to feel that for my whole life I had been standing on a precipice, that my loss had made me vulnerable, hard, and helpless; on knowing this I became overwhelmed with sadness and shame and pity for myself" (3-4). Xuela has much in common with Kincaid's younger protagonists, Annie John and Lucy Josephine Potter, except Xuela seems even more hurt and angry. And since all Kincaid's novels are semi-autobiographical, it is safe to assume that the emotions of her protagonists are a reflection of the author's own.[3]

In an interview with Donna Perry, Kincaid discussed *A Small Place*, her non-fiction work about Antigua, and she recalled that many reviewers found the book too angry. She told Perry, "I now consider anger a badge of honor. . . . I've really come to love anger. . . . I realized in writing that book that the first step to claiming yourself is anger. You get mad. And you can't do anything before you get angry. And I recommend getting very angry to everyone, anyone" (497-8). Anger is a catalyst for action, and action is a means of recovering what is lost: one's self, one's personal past, one's history. Kincaid told interviewer Moira Ferguson: "I have to make sense of my ancestral past—where I am from, my historical past, my group historical past, my group ancestry" (176). In *Annie John* and *Lucy*, Kincaid has attempted to recover her personal past, especially her troubled relationship with her mother and the country of her birth, Antigua. In *The Autobiography of My Mother*, the author has a more ambitious goal: to reclaim aspects of her historical past by examining such issues as European conquest, the plight of Africans and native populations in the Americas, and the cyclical nature of power relationships. Like AIDS activist Douglas Crimp, Kincaid has channeled her anger: "The development of my political consciousness and my ability to express it is really what you see" (Ferguson interview 167).

The "voice of loss" that Kincaid attempted to locate in the nameless narrator of "Ovando" has found more eloquent articulation in Xuela Claudette Richardson: "Everything about us is held in doubt and we the defeated define all that is unreal, all that is not human, all that is without love, all that is without mercy" (*Autobiography* 37). Although she is "one of the vanquished," during the course of the novel Xuela transforms herself into a godlike figure embodying the forces of life and death. She does this by harnessing the energy generated by her grief and rage over the loss of her mother. Although Xuela never saw her mother, she has a recurring dream of her mother's heels and the hem of her white dress as she descends a ladder. One time only, her mother sang a song in the dream: "it was only a song, but the sound of her voice was like a small treasure found in an abandoned chest, a treasure that inspires not astonishment but contentment and eternal pleasure" (31). Like Roland Barthes's photograph of his mother as a child, Xuela's memory of her mother's dream song allows her to sustain her sorrow for seventy-odd years, making it "the locus of [her] being in the present" (Woodward, "Late Theory" 95). The novel itself, Xuela's autobiography, is paradoxically her mother's story as well, for by claiming herself and recovering her own history, Xuela justifies her mother's brief existence.

Because her loss, her mother's death, has left Xuela "vulnerable, hard, and helpless," she is wary of love, "for love might give someone else the advantage" (48). Her father left her as an infant to be raised by his laundress. When she returns as a young girl to live with him, his new wife despises the offspring of his first marriage and apparently tries to murder her stepdaughter. Xuela rejoices in her stepmother's animosity: "She did not love me. I could see it in her face. My spirit rose to meet this challenge. No love: I could live in a place like this. I knew this atmosphere all too well. Love would have defeated me. Love would always defeat me" (29). As a young woman Xuela vows never to "allow the passage of time or the full weight of desire to make a pawn of me" (65). Even when she falls in love with the stevedore Roland, her basic distrust of all men— stemming from her ambiguous feelings for her corrupt policeman father— sabotages the relationship: "when [Roland] was lying on top of me he looked down at me as if I were the only woman in the world, the only woman he had ever looked at in that way—but that was not true, a man only does that when it is not true" (168).

Roland is married, but that is not the reason Xuela refuses to bear his child. She refuses to be a mother on principle. Granted, her first pregnancy occurred under less than ideal circumstances: her employer, a childless middle-aged woman, orchestrated an affair between her husband and Xuela in hope of a child that she could raise. Xuela purged her body of that child, nearly losing her own life in the process, and from that point onward she rejects motherhood: "I had never had a mother, I had just recently refused to become one, and I knew then that this refusal would be complete" (96). The novel provides mixed signals regarding Xuela's inability to bear children: mention of her "broken womb" (157) is contradicted by references to her fertility (175) and to conception (207). Yet there is no question that she equates childlessness with freedom; she even shares her knowledge of herbal "remedies" for pregnancy with other women: "I

had become such an expert at being ruler of my own life in this one limited regard that I could extend such power to any other woman who asked me for it"
(115).

Xuela's ability to deny life to the unborn endows her with godlike powers:

> I would never become a mother, but that would not be the same as
> never bearing children. I would bear children, but I would never be
> mother to them. I would bear them in abundance; they would emerge
> from my head, from my armpits, from between my legs; I would bear
> children, they would hang from me like fruit from a vine, but I would
> destroy them with the carelessness of a god. I would bear children in
> the morning, I would bathe them at noon in a water that came from my-
> self, and I would eat them at night, swallowing them whole, all at once.
> . . . It is in this way that I did not become a mother; it is in this way that
> I bore my children. (97-98)

In this passage, Xuela sounds very much like Lilith, Adam's first wife, turned
demon, whose rage and desire for vengeance made her a threat to all of Eve's
children.[4] Wonderful and terrible, Xuela defies convention and flies in the face
of social norms. Kincaid told Donna Perry: "really, when people say you're
charming you are in deep trouble. . . . I'm interested in being not a decent person" (498-9). And describing Xuela (as yet unnamed) to Moira Ferguson, Kincaid erases the boundary lines between her character and herself: "No, I think
actually the protagonist I am writing now, I have now, is perhaps lonely and
isolated, too—I think yes—and more godlike. There's hardly any point in writing about yourself as an agreeable fabulous person in your society. Why bother?
It would be very uninteresting" (187).

The passage from *The Autobiography of My Mother* quoted above marks
the turning point in Xuela's life, the point at which she decides to live completely on her own terms, to possess herself entirely, to be possessed by nothing
and no one. Earlier she had observed that a life without love was incomplete: "I
came to love myself in defiance, out of despair, because there was nothing else"
(56-57). Xuela takes possession of the only person she has ever loved, herself: "I
felt I did not want to belong to anyone, that since the one person I would have
consented to own me had never lived to do so, I did not want to belong to anyone; I did not want anyone to belong to me" (104). Like a conquistador laying
claim to a continent, Xuela takes possession of her own being: "The impulse to
possess is alive in every heart, and some people choose vast plains, some people
choose high mountains, some people choose wide seas, and some people choose
husbands; I choose to possess myself" (174). In this way Xuela reverses history,
and one of the vanquished becomes one of the victors: "in my defeat lies the
seed of my great victory, in my defeat lies the beginning of my great revenge"
(216).

Xuela marries her employer, an English doctor named Philip Bailey, even
though—or rather *because*—she does not love him: "I married a man I did not
love, but I would not have married a man I loved at all" (205). After Philip's

wife dies, addicted to "a most beautiful weed" that Xuela had introduced her to, Xuela takes possession of the adoring doctor in a reversal of European conquest: "Philip was of the conquering class. [My sister] was in awe of this, my own conquest—this was how she viewed it—and she despised me even more for it" (211). Xuela recognizes, as her sister does not, that this marriage is also "a kind of tragedy, a kind of defeat," for like all conquerors, she has found that domination of others diminishes the winners as well as the losers.

Like Jean Rhys's version of Edward Rochester in *Wide Sargasso Sea*, Philip is both victor and victim, heir to the spoils of Europe's imperial conquests, but cut off from some essential part of himself. At the end of Rhys's novel, Antoinette is her husband's prisoner, but he is permanently maimed by his wife's militant solipsism: "She had left me thirsty and all my life would be thirst and longing for what I had lost before I had found it" (172). Similarly, Xuela denies her English husband access to her world: "I blocked his entrance to the world in which he lived; eventually I blocked his entrance into all the worlds he had come to know. He became all the children I did not allow to be born" (224). Philip's predicament is significant, for it belies any simplistic binary opposition between victor and vanquished. Xuela acknowledges her own fascination with conquest and domination:

> Why should the world of adventure forever remain closed to me, the discovery of mountains, vast seas, miles upon miles of empty plains, the skies, the heavens, even cruel subordination of others? . . . The depths of evil, its results, were all too clear to me: its satisfactions, its rewards, the glorious sensations, the praise, the feeling of exaltation and superiority evil elicits when it is successful, the feeling of invincibility—I had observed all of this firsthand. All roads come to an end, and all ends are the same, trailing off into nothing; even an echo eventually will be silenced. (215)

These words echo Kincaid's remark to Moira Ferguson that the ebb and flow of power relationships over time is very complicated, that simply condemning the conquistadors is not an adequate response to the complexity of history: "I have to be in the position to bear in mind that they were wrong, and they could be me, and that is an ambivalence and that's what's complicated. At any moment you are anyone. You are the victim. You are the victor, at any moment" (184).

Xuela's marriage and Kincaid's remarks to Ferguson lend credence to what Michel Foucault describes as the cyclical nature of power relationships in human history:

> Humanity does not gradually progress from combat to combat until it arrives at universal reciprocity, where the rule of law finally replaces warfare; humanity installs each of its violences in a system of rules and thus proceeds from domination to domination. . . . The successes of history belong to those who are capable of seizing these rules, to replace those who had used them, to disguise themselves so as to pervert them, invert their meaning, and redirect them against those who had initially imposed them; controlling this complex mechanism, they will make it function so as to overcome the rulers through their own rules. (85-86)

Overcoming the rulers through their own rules: this is precisely how Jamaica Kincaid describes her education in the British colonial school system. Noting the influence on her work of Shakespeare, Wordsworth, Charlotte Brontë and Virginia Woolf, Kinciad tells Moira Ferguson: "But now I know a lot of things about language that I can use against the people who educated me very well" (175). However, Kincaid acknowledges the ironic complexity of her own existence as one of the vanquished who has turned the tables on Euro-America, whose success and affluence implicate her in the misdeeds of her adopted country: "We all do some pretty horrendous things. I contribute to pretty horrendous things. . . . I live in a nice house in a country that does pretty horrendous things" (183).

The complicated nature of power relationships extends even to Xuela's dead mother, who was of the Carib people. Though it is Xuela's genetic connection to these now nearly extinct native Americans that compels her to see herself as one of the defeated, in Columbus's time the Caribs were fierce warriors who played a part in the extermination of the peaceful Arawak Indians (Parry, Sherlock and Maingot 4). Kincaid observes: "The Caribs survived because they fought. They were fierce. Their whole stance had always been fighting. We would like to think the peaceful people survived, but they didn't" (Ferguson interview 173). She adds: "Hardly anyone has ever not done what [the conquistadors] did. Seen the advantage and said, 'you know, there are some helpless people over there and I can take advantage of it, but I am just not going to.' No one has ever done that" (183).

Xuela is of the Carib people, and like them she is a fighter. She is of the African people, and like them she is a survivor (*Autobiography* 16). She is of the European people, and like them she dreams of conquest and domination. Even as an old woman, Xuela derives sustenance from anger, loss, and grief; she takes pleasure in the memory of her victory and revenge. The speaker in one of Kincaid's early stories reflects on her childhood disappointments, which she refuses to relinquish: "My disappointments stand up and grow ever taller. They will not be lost to me. There they are. Let me pin tags on them. Let me have them registered, like newly domesticated animals" ("Wingless" 23-24). The sorrows and disappointments of life, and the losses and the pain, become for Kincaid and her protagonists the material from which they fashion their autobiographical narratives. Not for them the healing process of mourning: they need their grief and rage as a catalyst for the political act of claiming themselves in defiance of five hundred years of colonial history.

Notes

1. Discussing her work-in-progress in the 1994 interview, Jamaica Kincaid told Moira Ferguson how exciting it was to be writing for the first time "about a grown-up woman" who had lived "a full life" (187-188).

2. I have discussed senescence in two other novels by West Indian women writers in "Aging and Ageism in Paule Marshall's *Praisesong for the Widow* and Beryl Gilroy's *Frangipani House*."

3. In the Ferguson interview, Kincaid called *Annie John* and *Lucy* "very autobiographical" and described the novel she was working on (*The Autobiography of My Mother*) as "autobiographical in ideas, but not in situation." She added: "There is no reason for me to be a writer without autobiography. . . . I am someone who had to make sense of the past" (175-176).

4. According to Jewish legend, Lilith was the unnamed woman mentioned in the Bible (Gen. 1:27) before the creation of Eve. "She is popular today with feminists because she vigorously asserted her equality with Adam by virtue of their simultaneous creation, insisting, among other things, on being on top during sexual intercourse" (Siegel and Rheins 333). Lilith's anger, insubordination, and desire for revenge make her a fitting prototype for Xuela.

Works Cited

Blau, Herbert. "The Makeup of Memory in the Winter of Our Discontent." Woodward and Schwartz 13-36.

Erikson, Erik H., Joan M. Erikson, and Helen Q. Kivnick. *Vital Involvement in Old Age*. New York: W.W. Norton, 1986.

Ferguson, Moira. "A Lot of Memory: An Interview with Jamaica Kincaid." *The Kenyan Review* 16.1 (1994): 163-88.

Foucault, Michel. "Nietzsche, Genealogy, History." *The Foucault Reader*. Ed. Paul Rabinow. New York: Pantheon, 1984. 76-100.

George, Diana Hume. "'Who is the Double Ghost Whose Head is Smoke?' Women Poets on Aging." Woodward and Schwartz 134-53.

Kincaid, Jamaica. *The Autobiography of My Mother*. New York: Farrar, Straus and Giroux, 1996.

———. "Wingless." *At the Bottom of the River*. New York: Aventura-Vintage-Random House, 1985.

Parry, J.H. , Philip Sherlock, and Anthony Maingot. *A Short History of the West Indies*. 4th ed. London: Macmillan Caribbean, 1987.

Perry, Donna. "An Interview with Jamaica Kincaid." *Reading Black, Reading Feminist: A Critical Anthology*. Ed.

Gates Jr., Henry Louis. New York: Meridian-Penguin, 1990.

Rhys, Jean. *Wide Sargasso Sea*. 1966. New York: W.W. Norton, 1982.

Siegel, Richard, and Carl Rheins, comp. and ed. *The Jewish Almanac*. New York: Bantam, 1980.

Wilson, Lucy. "Aging and Ageism in Paule Marshall's *Praisesong for the Widow* and Beryl Gilroy's *Frangipani House*." *Journal of Caribbean Studies* 7:2-3 (1989-90): 189-199.

Woodward, Kathleen. "Late Theory, Late Style: Loss and Renewal in Freud and Barthes." *Aging and Gender in Literature*. Ed. Anne M. Wyatt-Brown and Janice Rossen. Charlottesville: University Press of Virginia, 1993.

———. "The Mirror Stage of Old Age." Woodward and Schwartz 97-113.

Woodward, Kathleen and Murray M. Schwartz, eds. *Memory and Desire: Aging, Literature, Psychoanalysis.* Bloomington: Indiana University Press, 1986.

PART TWO: Jean Rhys and the Sins of the Father

"Women Must Have Spunks": Jean Rhys's West Indian Outcasts

Since Wally Look Lai described *Wide Sargasso Sea* as "one of the genuine masterpieces of West Indian fiction" (17), quite a number of critics have focused on the Caribbean aspects of that novel, as well as *Voyage in the Dark* and several of Rhys's short stories. Louis James (111) and Mary Lou Emery (421), for example, have shown that Rhys's Caribbean concerns situate the intensely personal vision of her fiction within a much larger historical context. More specifically, Nancy Fulton has pointed to the parallels between black and white characters in *Wide Sargasso Sea* (344). Similarly, Helen Tiffin explains that Antoinette's suffering and enslavement by Edward Rochester reinforce her identification with the black Creole community (339), and Antoinette's ambiguous relationship with blacks has been explored by Charlotte Bruner as well (237).

Despite considerable critical attention to Jean Rhys's West Indian themes and characters, however, there has been relatively little focus on the black characters themselves. This is a significant oversight because two black West Indian characters—Selina Davis in "Let Them Call It Jazz" and Christophine Dubois, Antoinette's former nanny and only friend in *Wide Sargasso Sea*—are unique among Rhys's female characters. The "typical" Rhys protagonist, such as Anna Morgan or Antoinette Rochester, is a social outcast cut off from meaningful contact with other human beings. Abandoned but not free, she is powerless to alter her condition. Powerlessness, in fact, intensifies the misery of the social outcast for it cuts her off from the sources of pleasure, knowledge, and discourse that, according to Michel Foucault, are induced by the productive nature of power in society ("Truth and Power" 61).

But unlike Rhys's white protagonists, Selina and Christophine seem to thrive on adversity and to draw strength from their opposition to the prevailing power structures. Although no more a part of mainstream society than Anna or Antoinette, Selina and Christophine draw upon their inner resources and possess a kind of resiliency that their white West Indian counterparts lack. Furthermore, their insights into the uses and abuses of power in their respective societies reveal the full scope of Rhys's social vision as well as her commitment to truth, which places her at odds with centuries of erroneous beliefs and practices initiated and perpetuated in the interests of successive power groups.

Anna Morgan, the actress-turned-prostitute in *Voyage in the Dark*, and Antoinette-Bertha Rochester, the Creole heiress of *Wide Sargasso Sea* who becomes the mad prisoner of Thornfield Hall, are both West Indian by birth and victims by nature. Living in and near London in the 1930s and touring with a third-rate theatrical group, Anna falls prey to the machinations of a debonair insurance man, Walter Jeffries. Anna justifies her acceptance of money in exchange for sex on the grounds that she will "do anything for good clothes. Anything—anything for clothes" (22). This may seem callous, but the conditions of Anna's life—her youth and the fact that she is orphaned, exiled, and alone in a foreign land without financial or emotional support—alleviate the crassness of her materialistic aims. "In effect," explains Arnold Davidson, "Rhys uses her protagonist's naiveté as a lever to move the reader into unlikely judgments— judgments that do not simply reiterate the dictates of the society" (56). The structural device that reinforces Anna's naiveté and the reader's predisposition to be sympathetic is the juxtaposition of Anna's bleak, cold, English present with flashbacks to her sunny, warm, West Indian girlhood. It is in these memories that Anna comes closest to her nineteenth-century counterpart, Antoinette (nee Cosway) Mason Rochester.

For both Anna and Antoinette, the warmth and vibrant energy of the West Indies is epitomized in the lives of the black inhabitants of the islands. As a child, Anna spent many hours listening to Francine, the black cook, tell stories. Anna claims:

> I wanted to be black. I always wanted to be black. I was happy because Francine was there, and I watched her hand waving the fan backwards and forwards and the beads of sweat that rolled from underneath her handkerchief. Being black is warm and gay, being white is cold and sad. (27)

On the other hand, Antoinette, living in Jamaica just after the Emancipation Act was passed in 1838, is not as forthright in her identification with the black islanders, for she is very much aware that, as a member of the former slave-owning class, she is disdained by both the blacks and the newly rich whites who call her kind "white cockroach" and "white nigger." Despite the contempt and even physical harm that she and her family experience at the hands of the former slaves, the child Antoinette sees her own image in the face of Tia, a young black girl who had been her friend until racial tension came between them. As Antoinette's family estate is burned to the ground by an angry mob of former slaves, she turns to Tia for refuge:

> As I ran, I thought, I will live with Tia and I will be like her. Not to leave Coulibri. Not to go. Not. When I was close I saw the jagged stone in her hand but I did not see her throw it. I did not feel it either, only something wet, running down my face. I looked at her and saw her face crumple as she began to cry. We stared at each other, blood on my face, tears on hers. It was as if I saw myself. Like in a looking glass. (38)

The desire to be black, expressed by both Anna and Antoinette, is reiterated by Rhys herself in her unfinished autobiography, *Smile Please*:

> I have watched carnivals on television. They are doubtless very colourful but it seems to me that it is all planned and made up compared to the carnival I remember, when I used to long so fiercely to be black and to dance, too, in the sun, to that music. The carnival I knew has vanished. (43)

Rhys, like her protagonists, envies the black Creoles because they have "more freedom, particularly sexual, than the white islander who must conform to the constraints of the colonist" (Bruner 247). But the identification of white with black West Indian goes even deeper. Anna's desire to be black reveals her longing for "a racial heritage which seemed in natural harmony with life" (Staley 62) and a rejection of "European materialism in favor of the vitality of the black folk culture" (James 112).

Antoinette's ambiguous identification with Tia takes its final form at the conclusion of *Wide Sargasso Sea* when Tia appears to Antoinette in a dream and entices her to jump from the battlements of Thornfield Hall, now nearly engulfed by flames. Antoinette interprets this dream as a sign, and her ensuing destruction of Thornfield Hall has been compared to the "typical slave retaliation in the firing of the great house" (Tiffin 339). However, to see Antoinette's suicide as a triumphant assertion is to detract from the tragic implications of her life and violent death. Despite her imprisonment, Antoinette is not a slave: her own passivity brings her to England and leaves her with no options except death.

Nevertheless, critical response to Antoinette's suicide is consistently positive, even when qualified. Her death is seen as "her most decisive action and her final escape from domination" (Davidson 39), as a form of rebellion and assertion (James 124), as "a leap into the life she was never permitted to live" (Fulton 348), and even as a triumph over her surroundings (Wolf 152, Emery 428). I would argue, however, that Antoinette Rochester's suicide is no more a triumph than Anna Morgan's nearly fatal abortion at the end of *Voyage in the Dark*. These attempts to call Antoinette's desperate leap by any other name reveal a reluctance on the critics' part to accept her defeat, as if to do so would somehow diminish Rhys's remarkable achievement.

But this is not the case. Rhys has created the syntax and vocabulary needed to bridge the gap between the outcast and society, and her novels—especially *Wide Sargasso Sea*—give voice to the inarticulate anguish of solitude and rejection. Antoinette's demise is a tragedy, not a victory. It is the final act in a complex historical drama that pits those with power against those without. Both Anna Morgan and Antoinette Rochester are casualties of social and political conflicts that transcend the personal or sexual battles that each character is forced to wage. Although they identify with the black West Indians, their destinies more closely parallel the fate of the Caribs who, Anna recalls, "are now practically exterminated (*Voyage* 91). Antoinette *is* exterminated, and Anna's abortion symbolizes the end of her line of descent. Kenneth Ramchand maintains that the original inhabitants of the West Indies "were virtually eliminated" and today "are regarded as marginal to society" (164). The same could be said of Antoinette and Anna, one doomed to death by her own hand, the other to life in rented bed-sitting-rooms on the fringes of a hostile city.

However, Anna and Antoinette are not Rhys's final word on the subject of survival in a hostile environment. Significantly, it is two black characters who provide an alternative. An exile like Anna, Selina Davis, in "Let Them Call It Jazz," is a West Indian woman living in London. If anything, her situation is more tenuous than Anna's, for Selina is harassed by racists who despise not only her lilting foreign-sounding speech patterns but the color of her skin as well. She has been robbed of her life savings and evicted from her home, yet she still finds reason to sing and dance: "After I drink a glass or two I can sing and when I sing

all misery goes from my heart" (46). Selina is not one to suffer quietly or pas-
sively to acquiesce to her own oppression. After she throws a rock through the
window of an antagonistic neighbor, she asks herself: "Why I do that? It's not
like me. But if they treat you wrong over and over again the hour strike when
you burst out that's what" (55). The Holloway prison song, which Selina hears
from the courtyard below the punishment cells, epitomizes the spirit of the oppressed: "She was singing from the punishment cells, and she tell the girls
cheerio and never say die. . . . Some day I hear that song on trumpets and these
walls will fall and rest" (60-61).

Selina Davis stands bravely at the intersection of individual human freedom
and the power of institutional authority, yet frequently critical response to this
story has focused on the negative side of her situation: a "woeful portrait" one
critic calls it (Staley 126), while another aligns himself with Selina's neighbors
when he disparages her "foul talk" and "obscene dancing" (Wolfe 46). Louis
James is correct, though, when he observes that the white composer who steals
Selina's song cannot "take away what the song means to her, just as the exploitation of black music cannot remove the black sense of jazz" (115). "Never say
die" is the message of Selina's song, and its rhythm gives her the courage and
strength to go on living. Rhythm, claims West Indian novelist Wilson Harris,
provides the energy for civilization. He writes:

> Life, it would appear, realizes itself in potentiality and peril with the appear-
> ance of rhythm. . . . When the toy-man, the exploited man, becomes aware of
> original rhythms within the oppression of his world, contradictions are bared in
> a manner terrifying and yet containing the secret of change. (18-19)

For Selina, the secret of change is her discovery that she is "not frightened of
them any more—after all what else can they do?" (62)

How unlike her white West Indian counterparts is this high-spirited black
woman. Anna Morgan, for example, seems to drift through life in a semistupor.
Her friend Lauri warns her: "You always look half-asleep and people don't like
that" (*Voyage* 110). On another occasion, the masseuse Ethel Matthews exclaims: "You're not all there; you're a half-potty bastard. You're not all there;
that's what's the matter with you" (124). Anna's will has not been "crushed"
(Staley 67), for there is no evidence that she ever possessed an assertive nature.
And this is true as well of Antoinette, who accedes to her own exploitation and
debasement as the wife of Edward Rochester long before she even meets the
man. As a child Antoinette has a recurring and prophetic dream that she is walking in a forest with a man who hates her, yet she does not offer any resistance: "I
follow him, sick with fear but I make no effort to save myself; if anyone were to
try and save me, I would refuse. This must happen" (*Wide Sargasso Sea* 50). In
fact, years later two persons do try to save her, and Antoinette is good to her
word.

Antoinette's marriage having completely deteriorated, she turns for advice
to Christophine, who urges her to leave Edward. But when Antoinette argues
that she must stay because she will be laughed at and because she has no money,
Christophine cannot contain her indignation: "Why you ask me, if when I an-

swer you say no? Why you come up here if when I tell you the truth, you say no?" (90). At this critical moment, with Antoinette's happiness and ultimately her life in the balance, this free-thinking Creole girl, whose charm is in direct proportion to her identification with the mysteries of her West Indian homeland, suddenly adopts the racist, imperialist language of her husband and stepfather: "I stared at her, thinking, 'but how can she know the best thing for me to do, this ignorant, obstinate old negro woman, who is not certain if there is such a place as England'" (93). The ultimate betrayal in *Wide Sargasso Sea* is not Edward Rochester's agreeing to a loveless marriage for monetary gain, or even his infidelity with the servant girl Amelie; it is Antoinette's betrayal of her own heritage, the submersion of her West Indian identity in the rhetoric and attitudes of imperialism.

The second time Antoinette refuses the help of another who attempts to free her from the bonds of "English law" occurs when Sandi, her beloved black cousin, asks: "Will you come with me?" and Antoinette responds, "I cannot" (151). Why can she not? English law may have placed her inheritance in the hands of her husband, but marriage is not slavery: no one could stop her from walking away. Antoinette begins to resemble her predecessors in Rhys's earlier novels—Anna Morgan, Marya Zelli, Julia Martin, and Sasha Jansen—in her inability to choose personal integrity over financial dependency.

The most perceptive analysis of Antoinette's position is provided by Christophine, herself an outcast, a Martinican obeah woman who has spent the better part of her adult life living among Jamaicans who fear and envy her. Christophine has spent time in jail because of her obeah practice. Hers has not been an easy life, but she has the strength and resiliency that are so clearly lacking in her white mistresses, Antoinette and her mother, Annette. Christophine defies the powers that be and lives a full life on the fringes of respectable society:

> [Christophine] spat over her shoulder. "All women, all colours, nothing but fools. Three children I have. One living in this world, each one a different father, but no husband, I thank my God. I keep my money. I don't give it to no worthless man." (91)

Christophine has no patience for Antoinette's passivity. When Antoinette is immobilized by despair, Christophine admonishes her: "Get up, girl, and dress yourself. Women must have spunks to live in this wicked world" (84). Like Selina Davis and her "never say die" song, Christophine embodies the life force. When Antoinette was a child, it was Christophine who kept her family alive—despite Annette Cosway's death wish: "I dare say we would have died if she'd turned against us and that would have been a better fate. To die and be forgotten and at peace. Not to know that one is abandoned, lied about, helpless" (19).

The shift in power, as a result of the Emancipation Act, from the former slave owners to the newly rich whites, is the cause of Annette's despair and the Cosway family's social descent. But to Christophine, the abolishment of slavery is a source of contemptuous amusement:

> No more slavery! She had to laugh! "These new ones have Letter of the Law. Same thing. They got magistrate. They got fine. They got jail house and chain gang. They got tread machine to mash up people's feet. New ones worse than old ones—more cunning, that's all." (22-23)

Christophine is nobody's fool. She has an intuitive grasp of the subtle ebb and flow of power in Jamaican society. In a few short sentences she captures the essence of what Michel Foucault describes as "the endlessly repeated play of dominations":

> Humanity does not gradually progress from combat to combat until it arrives at universal reciprocity, where the rule of law finally replaces warfare; humanity installs each of its violences in a system of rules and thus proceeds from domination to domination. . . . The successes of history belong to those who are capable of seizing these rules, to replace those who had used them, to disguise themselves so as to pervert them, invert their meaning, and redirect them against those who had initially imposed them; controlling this complex mechanism, they will make it function so as to overcome the rulers through their own rules. ("Nietzsche" 85-86)

Rhys's former slave owners have, in fact, been overcome through their own rules: "old time white people nothing but white nigger now, and black nigger better than white nigger," Tia proclaims to Antoinette the last time they play together as friends (21). Christophine is not impressed by talk of the Emancipation for she recognizes a new form of tyranny in the "Letter of the Law" and a new breed of tyrant in the professional classes and the police: "That doctor an old-time doctor. These new ones I don't like them. First word in their mouth is police. Police—that's something I don't like" (125).

To appreciate fully Christophine's incisive analysis of Jamaican society after the abolition of slavery, it is helpful to compare it with that of Douglass Hall, taken from a paper he read at the Royal Institute for International Affairs in London two years *after* the first publication of *Wide Sargasso Sea*. According to Hall:

> The abolition of slavery ostensibly removed the legal supports of these [class] divisions. After August 1, 1838, all were equal citizens—in the eyes of the law. But all were not equal in the eyes of society or in the eyes of those who were the makers and the administrators of the law. . . . Slavery as a legal institution had gone; but the society shaped by slavery remained with its criteria of whiteness, wealth, and education. (8)

Because she is black, poor, and wanted by the police, Christophine is as powerless to alter the tragic course of Antoinette's life as she is to redress social and political injustice in nineteenth-century Jamaica. But as a narrative device, Christophine represents Jean Rhys's unequivocal assertion of defiance in the face of injustice and coercion. This defiant stance places Jean Rhys in the ranks of other socially committed writers, like Michel Foucault, whose insight into power and its abuses closely parallels Rhys's own, less systematic social theorizing.

Not long before she died, Rhys told novelist David Plante that as a child, living in the small West Indian island of Dominica, she had been called "socialist Gwen" because she had taken the side of the blacks and the workers against the white ruling class. She pleaded with Plante to "tell the truth" in the face of all the lies: "You must tell the truth about them. . . . You must tell the truth against their lies" (50). Rhys's white protagonists are passive victims of society's injustice. But Rhys herself, like Selina Davis and Christophine Dubois, could not be coerced into self-betrayal. In a dialogue with herself, Rhys describes her writing as "dangerous" because of the madness that others perceive in her. "But if everything is in me," she reasons, "good, evil and so on, so must strength be in me if I know how to get at it" (*Smile Please* 133). Strength through knowledge: this is Rhys's legacy to an unjust world.

Rhys intuited that her thought and writing were "dangerous" to the establishment. Foucault, echoing Nietzsche and Artaud, articulates a similar insight when he gives the lie to the myth that "historical consciousness is neutral, devoid of passions, and committed solely to the truth." Rather, as a manifestation of "the will to knowledge," historical consciousness "discovers the violence of a position that encourages the dangers of research and delights in disturbing discoveries" ("Nietzsche" 95). Whereas Rhys was implicitly political, Foucault was overtly so. He saw political responsibility as the highest duty of the intellectual, whose task "is to criticize the working of institutions. . . . to criticize them in such a manner that the political violence which has always exercised itself obscurely through them will be unmasked, so that one can fight them" (qtd. in Rabinow 6).

Power and powerlessness, discourse and silence, prisoners, patients, and the machinery that keeps society functioning: these are the dominant concerns addressed by Jean Rhys. These are Foucault's concerns as well, and the similarity is significant. Rhys would agree with Foucault that the "battle for truth" is "not a matter of a battle 'on behalf' of truth, but a battle about the status of truth and the economic role it plays" ("Truth and Power" 132). Rhys reveals her own awareness of the arbitrary relationship between truth and power through Christophine's insight into history's succession of dominations, each touting its version of "Truth" and "Letter of the Law."

But the courage and strength exhibited by Christophine and Selina merely emphasize the weakness of Rhys's white protagonists who, though sympathetically portrayed, leave the reader feeling oddly unmoved precisely *because* of their passivity and detachment. Detachment from history is simply the converse of passive submission to it; neither is an adequate response to the social, economic, and cultural challenges that face mankind. Rhys accepted the challenge by writing "dangerous" books. Had she shirked her responsibility, Rhys felt that she would "not have earned death" (*Smile Please* 133). Moreover, she would not have earned a place next to Nietzsche, Artaud, Foucault, and other radical thinkers who dared to challenge the comforting lies, passing as articles of faith, that throughout history have drawn the line between those who dominate and those who are dominated.

Works Cited

Bruner, Charlotte H. "A Caribbean Madness: Half Slave and Half Free." *Canadian Review of Comparative Literature* 11 (1984): 236-248.

Davidson, Arnold E. *Jean Rhys.* New York: Ungar, 1985.

Emery, Mary Lou. "The Politics of Form: Jean Rhys's Social Vision in *Voyage in the Dark* and *Wide Sargasso Sea.*" *Twentieth Century Literature* 28 (1982): 418-430.

Foucault, Michel. "Nietzsche, Genealogy, History." Rabinow 76-100.

———. "Truth and Power." Rabinow 51-75.

Fulton, Nancy J. Casey. "Jean Rhys's *Wide Sargasso Sea*: Exterminating the White Cockroach." *Revista Interamericana* 4 (1974): 340-349.

Hall, Douglas. "The Colonial Legacy in Jamaica." *New World Quarterly* 4.3 (1968): 7-22.

Harris, Wilson. "The Question of Form and Realism in the West Indian Artist." *Tradition, the Writer and Society.* London: New Beacon, 1967. 13-20.

James, Louis. "Sun Fire—Painted Fire: Jean Rhys as a Caribbean Novelist." *ARIEL* 8 (1977): 111-127.

Lai, Wally Look. "The Road to Thornfield Hall." Rev. of *Wide Sargasso Sea. New World Quarterly* 4.2 (1968): 17-27.

Plante, David. *Difficult Women. A Memoir of Three.* New York: Atheneum, 1983.

Rabinow, Paul, ed. *The Foucault Reader.* New York: Pantheon, 1984.

———. Introduction. Rabinow 3-29.

Ramchand, Kenneth. *The West Indian Novel and Its Background.* 2nd ed. London: Heinemann, 1983.

Rhys, Jean. "Let Them Call it Jazz." 1960. *Tigers are Better-Looking.* New York: Penguin, 1981.

———. *Smile Please: An Unfinished Autobiography.* Berkeley: Creative Arts/Ellis, 1979.

———. *Voyage in the Dark.* 1934. New York: Penguin, 1980.

———. *Wide Sargasso Sea.* 1966. New York: Penguin, 1980.

Staley, Thomas F. *Jean Rhys: A Critical Study.* Austin: University of Texas Press, 1979.

Tiffin, Helen. "Mirror and Mask: Colonial Motif in the Novels of Jean Rhys." *World Literature Written in English* 17 (1978): 328-341.

Wolfe, Peter. *Jean Rhys.* Boston: Twayne, 1980.

European or Caribbean: Jean Rhys and the Language of Exile

> They bore within their breasts the grief
>   That fame can never heal—
> The deep, unutterable woe
>   Which none save exiles feel.
> (W.E. Aytoun, *The Island of the Scots*, xii)

The question of identity in Jean Rhys's life and fiction is inextricably bound to the condition of exile that shaped her perceptions and those of her characters. Rhys was truly a woman without a country. England, where she lived for most of her adult life, was a cold, unreceptive place for the writer. Recognition came too late to compensate for a lifetime of loneliness and financial difficulty. The question of Rhys's West Indian roots is even more problematic. The daughter of a Welsh father and a white Creole mother, Rhys felt exiled even before she moved to England because she was cut off from the black community in Dominica (Jordis 159). Thus Rhys suffered from what Amon Saba Saakana describes as "the mental condition of double alienation" (Saakana 161). Doubly dispossessed, Jean Rhys differs from black West Indian exiles who, as George Lamming points out, "could never have felt the experience of being in a minority" (33).

Jean Rhys is both Prospero *and* Caliban, a descendant of white colonizers but also, as a woman, colonized and excluded by the patriarch's language. "Carib Indian and African slave, both seen as the wild fruits of Nature, share equally that spirit of revolt which Prospero by sword or language is determined to conquer" (Lamming 13). In her own way, Rhys also shares that revolutionary spirit: she wrests Prospero's language from him, inverts and subverts it in her fiction, and turns the empty space between the two worlds into a privileged place, the exile's domain, by means of what Edward Said calls a "contrapuntal" awareness.

Exile and Literature

The uniquely literary nature of exile has been examined by Said, Andrew Gurr, and Michael Seidel, among others. According to Gurr, exile has had an "enormously constructive" effect on writers who were born in the colonies and fled to the metropolis, since it creates in them "a stronger sense of home" and thus "a clearer sense of [their] own identity" than is available to their metropolitan counterparts (9). Questioning this essentially romantic view, Said writes: "To think of exile as beneficial, as a spur to humanism or to creativity, is to belittle its mutilations. . . . For exile is fundamentally a discontinuous state of being. Exiles are cut off from their roots, their land, their past" (50-51). Yet Said recognizes the literary nature of exile, in that the unreality of the exile's new world resembles fiction. Furthermore, the exile's double or contrapuntal vision can lead to a restored and enhanced identity and even a more meaningful life.[1]

Michael Seidel similarly views the exilic condition as a paradigm for narrative strategy:

> for narrative performs not only as an experimental rival but as an aesthetic substitute or supplement. Exilic imagining in this sense is both the mirror and the "other" of narrative process; mimesis becomes an alien (or allegorical) phenomenon that establishes fictional sovereignty on fictional ground. . . . The narrative imagination inhabits exilic domain where absence is presence, or, to put it the other way around, where presence is absence. (198-9)

While Seidel focuses "on exile as an enabling fiction" and not on the actual conditions or politics of exile, the autobiographical nature of Jean Rhys's fiction accommodates such a double perspective.[2] And the purely aesthetic concerns expressed by Seidel do not address the real pathos of exile, the extent to which exiles, and women in particular, are often relegated to a position of powerlessness in their adopted land. This is the essence of Jean Rhys's vision. In her novels and stories, matters of race, gender, class, and ethnicity are intensified by the contrapuntal vision of exile, which highlights the interplay of power structures within British, West Indian, and Continental societies.

The Irreconcilable Worlds of "Voyage in the Dark"

Counterpoint is the main structuring device employed in *Voyage in the Dark*, which juxtaposes Anna Morgan's bright, warm memories of her West Indian past against the bleak present, London: "hundreds thousands of white people rushing along and the dark houses frowning down one after the other all alike all stuck together—the streets like smooth shut-in ravines and the dark houses frowning down" (Rhys 9). In this passage, repetition, alliteration, internal rhyme, and additive syntax reflect the mind-numbing effect that the environment has on Anna. But if England seems unreal to Anna, so do Dominica's green hills, sea smell, dark cliffs, and ravines: "Sometimes it was as if I were back there and as if England were a dream. At other times England was the real thing and out there was the dream, but I could never fit them together" (8).

Because these two worlds tend to cancel each other out, Anna is left suspended, floating in a semi-trance from one sexual encounter to the next. As characters, events, and locations become more tedious and diffuse, language itself moves to the forefront, focusing the reader's attention on idiosyncrasies in the characters' word choices. In the following exchange between Anna and Walter Jeffries, his thinly disguised misogyny begins to surface:

> "Vincent's coming down by train tomorrow and bringing a girl. I thought it might be fun."
> "Oh, is he?" I said. "How nice. Is she the girl I met—Eileen?"
> "No, not Eileen. Another girl." (76)

Some months later, Anna imagines a man she slept with bragging about the encounter:

> "I picked up a girl in London and she. . . . Last night I slept with a girl who . . ."
> That was me.
> Not 'girl' perhaps. Some other word, perhaps. Never mind. (157)

This is Prospero's language—coercive, demeaning, excluding. To Walter, Vincent's female companion is a "girl" even though he later insists that she "is old for a woman" (87). Anna cringes at the thought of being "a girl in London" or, worse, "a tart," but she defuses that epithet in the following exchange with Joe Adler:

> He didn't say anything for a bit and then he said, "Why do you go around with Laurie? Don't you know she's a tart?"
> "Well," I said, "why shouldn't she be a tart? It's just as good as anything else, as far as I can see." (127)

Anna similarly defuses the word "virgin" by insisting that virginity "doesn't matter anyway. . . . People have made all that up" (36). Having lost her virginity, Anna thinks, "I am bad, not good any longer, bad. That has no meaning, absolutely none. Just words. But something about the darkness of the streets has a meaning" (57).

Sexist language has "no meaning" because "people" have arbitrarily assigned significance to these terms. But "the darkness of the streets," Anna's voyage into the underworld of cheap hotels and drunken encounters with strange men—*that* has meaning, because the underworld descent "is one of the most profound narrative models for the exilic experience in literature. . . . Descent is that ending which is also a telling, that exile which conjures up imaginable territory" (Seidel 13). Anna's brush with death after her abortion is the culmination of her exilic experience, annexing as it does absolute otherness—the laughing hag (Rhys 152, 187) and the bald-headed dwarf (165) of her nightmares—to the England of Anna's present and the island paradise of her past. Anna's return to consciousness and physical health—"Ready to start all over again in no time, I've no doubt" (187)—is an ironic inversion of the hero's triumphant return to society.[3]

War and Exile in Three Short Stories

While Anna's voyage into the dark night of the soul infuses even the most mimetic elements of the novel with allegorical significance, such is not the case in two of Rhys's short stories, where exile's privileged perspective, combined with a semi-documentary style, reconstructs an image of Europe after World War I that in some ways resembles Christopher Isherwood's pre-World War II Germany in *The Berlin Stories*, especially the distanced yet nonjudgmental point of view that distinguishes both authors' vignettes. In "Vienne," England displaces Dominica as the "absent presence," for this story parallels experiences in

Rhys's life that occurred several years after the events recalled in *Voyage in the Dark*. The pregnant narrator, Francine, and her husband Pierre are thinly disguised versions of Rhys and her first husband, Jean Lenglet, when they lived on the Continent during the years following the Great War, an exciting time when many people were involved in the dangerous but highly profitable business of currency exchange.[4]

Francine's exilic perspective approaches the "scrupulous subjectivity" described by Edward Said as the ideal stance for the exile:

> If the exile is neither going to rush into an uncritical gregariousness nor sit on the sidelines nursing a wound, he or she must cultivate a scrupulous (not indulgent or sulky) subjectivity. . . . For there is considerable merit to the practice of noting discrepancies between various concepts and ideas and what they actually produce. (54)

But "Vienne" is one of Rhys's early stories, and as such it is tainted by "uncritical gregariousness." A Japanese officer is a "poor dear" and an English translator a "marvelous person!" (112). There is an indulgent chattiness to Francine's insistence—"I mustn't cry, I won't cry" (108)—that is absent from a much later version of this episode in "Temps Perdi," and a comparison of these two stories attests to the development and refinement of Jean Rhys's contrapuntal or exilic vision over a period of approximately forty years. A third story, "I Spy a Stranger," from the same period as "Temps Perdi," shows how the subject of misogyny accrues added political significance with the advent of World War II. All three stories overlap in terms of Rhys's life experiences, and consequently, when examined together, they disclose the exilic imagination as it develops both in historic time and in narrative space.[5]

In "Vienne" and "Temps Perdi," misogyny is seen as a common denominator among the German, the Japanese, and the English officers who frequent Sacher's Hotel in Vienna during the summer of 1921. In the earlier story, Francine explains with characteristic directness that:

> Hato [a Japanese officer] was a great joy. He despised Europeans heartily. They all did that, exception made in favor of Germany—for the Japanese thought a lot of the German army and the German way of keeping women in their place. They twigged that at once. Not much they didn't twig. (96)

When Rhys retells this story in "Temps Perdi," a Japanese officer's affinity for Germanic misogyny is presented less directly. The nameless narrator recalls the typist Simone's reconstruction of Captain Yoshi's confidences:

> "Well," I said, "He looked as if he were telling you all his secrets."
> "He was," Simone said, "he was. Do you know what he was saying? He was saying how much he admires the Germans. He said they'll soon have the best army in Europe, and that they'll dominate it in a few years. . . . He said the French love women too much. He said only the Germans know how to treat women. The Germans and the English think the same way about women, he

said, but the French think differently. He said the English and the French together won't last another year, and they are splitting up already." (264-5)

Although less direct in terms of narrative structure, the "Temps Perdi" passage
is more far-reaching than the one from "Vienne," since at a distance of forty
years Rhys associates the Germans' attitude towards women with their later attempt to dominate Europe militarily.

There are other significant differences between the two stories. The youthful Francine in "Vienne" has internalized Prospero's attitudes; she uses the language of the patriarchy when she describes women in terms of their "podgy
hands," "thick ankles," and "enormous" feet—women being equal to the sum of
their bodily parts (101). Her goal for her own appearance is to achieve a doll-
like look by means of make-up and "stuff dropped in [her eyes] to make the pu-
pils big and black" (108). The much older narrator in "Temps Perdi" recalls her
youthful preoccupation with pretty dresses, but the passages critical of other
women's appearance have been expunged.

Rhys launches a direct attack on misogyny in "I Spy a Stranger," which is
also written in the first person, although the character who corresponds to Francine of "Vienne" and the nameless narrator of "Temps Perdi" is here not the
narrator but rather her cousin Laura. Like Francine, Laura has lived in Central
Europe, returning to England only when she was "forced to" (244). In her exercise-book, Laura writes about being unable "to bear the comments on what had
happened in Europe . . . the eternal question of who let down who, and when"
(248), a passage that recalls Francine's despair when Pierre admits "that he had
lost money—other people's money—the Commission's money—Ishima had let
him down" (114). Laura's cousin, Marion Hudson, is pressed by her husband
and her irate neighbors to expel Laura from the Hudson household and force her
to return to London, now that the blitz is over. Laura's unsociable, bookish
ways, but especially her Central European connections, have turned public opin-
ion against her. Laura is suspected of "trying to pass information on to the en-
emy," and her exercise-book is confiscated by the police as evidence (250).

While the exercise-book reveals no evidence that Laura is a spy, it does
contain the most blistering condemnation of English misogyny to be found in all
of Rhys's fiction. Laura recalls:

> those endless, futile arguments we used to have when we all knew the worse
> was coming to the worst. The world dominated by Nordics, German version—
> what a catastrophe. But if it were dominated by Anglo-Saxons, wouldn't that be
> a catastrophe too? Then, of course, England and the English. . . . There is some-
> thing strange about their attitude to women as women. Not dislike (or fear).
> That isn't strange of course. But it's all so completely taken for granted, and
> surely that is strange. It has settled down and become an atmosphere, or, if you
> like, a climate, and no one questions it, least of all the women themselves.
> There is *no* opposition. The effects are criticized, for some of the effects are
> hardly advertisements for the system, the cause is seldom mentioned, and then
> very gingerly. The few mild ambiguous protests usually come from men. Most
> of the women seem to be carefully trained to revenge any unhappiness they feel
> on each other, or on children—or on any individual man who happens to be at a

disadvantage. In dealing with men as a whole, a streak of subservience, of ser-
vility, usually appears, something cold, calculating, lacking in imagination. But
no one can go against the spirit of a country with impunity, and propaganda
from the cradle to the grave can do a lot. (248)

Laura amuses herself in the exercise-book by inventing titles for future books:

> *Woman an Obstacle to the Insect Civilization? The Standardization of Woman,
> The Mechanization of Woman . . . Misogyny and British Humour . . . Misogyny
> and War, The Misery of Woman and the Evil of Men or the Great Revenge that
> Makes all other Revenges Look Silly.* (249)

Through Laura, Jean Rhys has aligned herself with Caliban, with the black
slave and the Carib Indian who have been "colonized by language, and excluded
by language" (Lamming 15). In England, Rhys, like George Lamming's exiled
Caliban,

> does not feel the need to understand an Englishman, since all relationships be-
> gin with an assumption of previous knowledge, a knowledge acquired in the
> absence of the people known. This relationship with the English is only another
> aspect of the West Indian's relation to the *idea* of England. (Lamming 25)

Rhys's "*idea* of England" is complicated by the fact that in her life and her fiction, England represents both the "present absence"—in *Voyage in the Dark*,
Anna Morgan's dark, frowning London house "all alike all stuck together"—and
the "absent presence"—Francine's imagined place of refuge from the terrifying
events that force her and Pierre to flee from Hungary when Pierre's misman-
agement of other people's money gets them in trouble with the law. Anna, exiled in England, longs for the West Indies; Francine, adrift in Central Europe,
insists: "We must go to London" (Rhys, *Collected Short Stories* 120). Pierre
warns her not to count on help from her English friends, but Francine persists.
As the two later stories reveal, Pierre was right. For the older version of Francine in "Temps Perdi," England is "the land of the dead" (257); and in "I Spy a
Stranger," Laura has discovered that "coming back to England was the worst
thing [she] could have done, that almost anything else would have been preferable" (247).

England, for Jean Rhys, was "perhaps the greatest disappointment of her
life and one she never stopped resenting" (Annan 154). But as an emblem of the
exilic condition, the *idea* of England plays a crucial role in the unfolding of
Rhys's contrapuntal vision. Like *Voyage in the Dark*, "Temps Perdi" juxtaposes
England and the West Indies, though structurally the works are quite different.
Whereas Anna Morgan's West Indian memories and English experiences overlap in the text as in her mind, the narrator in "Temps Perdi" separates her experiences in England, on the Continent, and in the West Indies. In the process,
she travels through time and space to a mythical place where women speak a
secret language.

An Alternative to Prospero's Language

Section One of "Temps Perdi" is itself divided into two time frames. The narrator, apparently fairly advanced in years, recalls her stay, at some point in her past, in an English country house whose coldness in turn reminds her of Vienna. Section One thus slips gracefully into the second section—"The Sword Dance and the Love Dance"—set in Vienna shortly after World War I. Section Two ends with the narrator's remark that the liberating effect of memory will turn her into "a savage person—a real Carib" (*Collected Short Stories* 267). This phrase provides the transition into Section Three: "Carib Quarter."

The third section describes the narrator's brief return visit to the West Indies and to an estate called Temps Perdi,[6] which in the Creole patois "does not mean, poetically, lost or forgotten time, but, matter-of-factly, wasted time, lost labor" (*Collected Short Stories* 267). This section contains both: the "wasted" effort of the narrator's disappointing visit to Salybia, the Carib Quarter, and the "lost" time of a (probably apocryphal) account of the "original West Indians," who presumably inhabited the islands before the Caribs came from the South American mainland and the Spaniards from Europe. According to a book once read by the narrator, the male members of this aboriginal people were killed by the Spaniards and the Caribs, or deported to Haiti:

> But the book, written by an Englishman in the 1880s, said that some of the women, who had survived both the Spaniards and the Caribs . . . had carried on the old language and traditions, handing them down from mother to daughter. This language was kept a secret from their conquerors, but the writer of the book claimed to have learned it. (270)

Local West Indian custom holds that Carib women have inherited this "language that the men don't know" (269).

Despite the narrator's disclaimer regarding the nineteenth-century author's excess of imagination, this idea of an all-female aboriginal language is emblematic of the exile's true "home"—a language untainted by Prospero's because it predates the white man's rule. The language of the patriarchy reinforces the distance between persons of different race, creed, class, or sex. Even within a group, feelings of difference and hostility are maintained by means of language, as in the distinction made throughout *Voyage in the Dark* between women and girls, ladies and tarts, virgins and non-virgins. By keeping women divided among themselves, the language of Prospero protects its interests. But the secret language of the Carib women has had the opposite effect: it has forged a bond among women that has survived incursions from two continents, linking generations of mothers and daughters in a conspiracy of eloquent silence.

Whether this secret language does or ever did exist among the Carib women is beside the point; its significance within the context of Jean Rhys's life and work should be clear. Toward the end of "Temps Perdi", the narrator lies "caged under a mosquito net" thinking: "Now I am home, where the earth is sometimes red and sometimes black. Round about here is ochre—a Carib skin" (274).

Rhys's home is neither the West Indies of her "lost" childhood nor the England of her many and sometimes "wasted" adult years. Home for Jean Rhys is a language like "a Carib skin," a mosquito net of language that protects and confines the writer, "a prisoner in a cell of small peepholes" (274). Safe within the Carib body of her text, Jean Rhys is also limited by her exilic condition. A white girl in a black society that she envied and longed to be a part of, a West Indian in the imperial English system that reinforced her sense of powerlessness both as a colonial and as a woman: Rhys perceived both worlds as though from a very great distance and felt herself cut off from other people.[7] But this contrapuntal point of view is for Rhys, as it is for Edward Said and other exiles, a source of power and inspiration: "Exiles cross borders, break barriers of thought and experience. . . . Seeing 'the entire world as a foreign land' makes possible originality of vision" (54-55).

*   *   *

In a poem about the novelist, Derek Walcott describes the child Jean Rhys, whose sigh transcends the barriers between two cultures:

> And the sigh of the child
> is white as an orchid
> on a crusted log
> in the bush of Dominica,
> a V of Chinese white
> meant for the beat of seagull
> over a sepia souvenir of Cornwall,
> as the white hush between two sentences. (428)

A fragile white flower of the Caribbean transplanted to the cold brown English soil, Jean Rhys made her home in neither place. Rather, she lived and continues to thrive in a linguistic space, the "white hush between two sentences."

Notes

1. Said's differentiation among exiles, refugees, expatriates, and *émigrés* is not pertinent to my study. Although Rhys was not "banished" from the West Indies or from England, she was an exile nonetheless, by virtue of history, circumstances, race, and gender.
2. In a review of Rhys's autobiography, *Smile Please*, Gabriele Annan calls Rhys "one of the most autobiographical novelists there has ever been" (154). Thus it is nearly impossible, and very likely counterproductive, to maintain a rigid demarcation between the author's life and the events described in her fiction.
3. In *Wide Sargasso Sea*, Antoinette's madness is another variation on the underworld descent, and, like Anna's voyage, it is a profoundly ironic inversion of the motif. For a more detailed discussion of both of these novels, see my article

"'Women Must Have Spunks': Jean Rhys's West Indian Outcasts," *Modern Fiction Studies*, no. 32 (Autumn 1986), pp. 439-48.

4. According to Thomas Staley, fragments of Rhys's post-war years on the Continent "appear throughout her work, from *The Left Bank* (1927) to *Tigers are Better Looking* (1968)"; and some of the events surrounding Rhys's and Lenglet's "flight from Middle-Europe are described in the short story 'Vienne'" (*Jean Rhys: A Critical Study,* Austin: University of Texas Press, 1979, pp. 8, 9).

5. "Vienne" was originally published in *The Left Bank* in 1927. "Temps Perdi" and "I Spy a Stranger" were published in 1969 in *Penguin Modern Stories*. All three have been reprinted in *Jean Rhys: The Collected Short Stories*.

6. *Vide* Staley, p. 16, who notes that Rhys returned to Dominica only once, for a two month-long visit in 1936.

7. In *Smile Please*, Rhys recalls a lonely Christmas day in a rented bed-sitting room: "I would never be a part of anything. I would never really belong anywhere, and I knew it, and all my life would be the same, trying to belong, and failing. Always something would go wrong. I am a stranger and I always will be, and after all I don't really care." (Berkeley: Donald S. Ellis/Creative Arts, 1979, pp. 99-100.)

Works Cited

Annan, Gabriele. "Turned Away by the Tropics." *Times Literary Supplement*, December 21, 1979.

Gurr, Andrew. *Writers in Exile: The Identity of Home in Modern Literature*. Atlantic Highlands, New Jersey: Humanities Press, 1981.

Jordis, Christine. "Jean Rhys ou la perspective de l'exil." *Nouvelle Revue Francaise*, July-August, 1983: 156-167.

Lamming, George. *The Pleasures of Exile*. London: Michael Joseph, 1960.

Rhys, Jean. *The Collected Short Stories*. New York: W.W. Norton, 1987.

———. *Voyage in the Dark*. 1934. New York: W.W. Norton, 1982.

Saakana, Amon Saba. *The Colonial Legacy in Caribbean Literature*. Trenton: Africa World Press, 1987.

Said, Edward. "The Mind of Winter: Reflections on Life in Exile." *Harper's Magazine*, September 1984: 49-55.

Seidel, Michael. *Exile and the Narrative Imagination*. New Haven: Yale University Press, 1986.

Walcott, Derek. "Jean Rhys." *Collected Poems* 1948-1984. New York: Farrar Strauss Giroux, 1986.

Helen of the Culture Wars: Jean Rhys and the Critics

The role of race in Jean Rhys's fiction and in her life is complex, fraught with ambiguity and laden with historical implications. Little wonder that Jean Rhys criticism has sometimes been the locus of tension and misunderstanding. I myself was conscripted into what Kamau Brathwaite refers to as "the great Eurocritical armada" (Brathwaite 78) when Peter Hulme mentioned my name in his 1994 overview of critical writing about *Wide Sargasso Sea* (Hulme 9). According to Elaine Savory, Hulme incurred the wrath of Brathwaite by citing comments Brathwaite made in his 1974 *Contradictory Omens*, without taking into account the cultural climate from which Brathwaite's book emerged (Savory, *Jean Rhys* 217). In his 1995 response to Hulme's essay, Brathwaite blasts *"the critical stance that things now OK & can therefore be written about from the point of view of neo-appropriation . . . which is what the whole wash of books on Rhys at least in Hulme's reading appears to thrive on—a false or NO knowledge of Caribb (or 'creole') 'reality' . . . so that Rhys becomes a kind of wishful metaphor for what these critics want to 'say', & a way of masking any element of GUILT"* (Brathwaite 73, ellipses added). Rhys, according to Brathwaite, "has become the Helen of the [culture] wars" (77) between West Indian writers/critics and outsiders *"who now seek to use her in their Caribbean &/or postcolonial &/or womanist &/or wonderland paradigms"* (76).

Brathwaite's witty, acerbic response to Hulme does not exclude Europeans, Americans and others from the table, but he sets some conditions for our participation in Caribbean discourse. Emphasizing that his work *"has never even **hinted** at any form of cultural or other apartheid—quite the contrary,"* Brathwaite continues: *"so all my work starts from my yard while trying to speak to you in yours; but this predicates that you will be DOING THE SAME THING: speaking to me from yr yard & LISTENING w / this understanding to me as I try to be listening w / understanding to you"* (75).

Commenting on the clash between Hulme and Brathwaite, Elaine Savory makes the following observation:

> The chasm between cultural locations and their corresponding intellectual visions is very clear here: Hulme seemed to desire a scholarly space beyond race for literary discussion; Brathwaite's reply implied as an ideal a society where the races are politically equal but each conscious of history, free to speak about it and fully aware of the ways each influences the other, a society not yet realised, even in the Caribbean. (219)

Although Brathwaite's ideal society is as yet unrealized, several essays and books, including Savory's, have brought Jean Rhys scholarship somewhat closer to the goal by dealing candidly with racial consciousness in Rhys's fiction and life, and by attempting to situate Rhys in relation to the troubled history of the Caribbean region. According to Savory, Rhys's "construction of black society was part of a private fantasy . . . she sometimes longed to cross over, making of the black community an image of all she felt she lacked" (29). This strain of modernist primitivism was hardly unique to Jean Rhys, but as a white Creole descended on her mother's side from slaveholders, "Rhys was born into a morally bizarre world . . . a world in which her colour and status marked her as culpable and in which the idea, learned from Catholicism, of confession and forgiveness may have seemed at times impossible in the sight of history" (Savory 110).

In *Jean Rhys's Historical Imagination*, Veronica Marie Gregg also attempts to situate Jean Rhys historically, on the grounds that "[t]he *historical and discursive processes* through which the Creole subjectivity is construed forms one of the most significant aspects of her writing" (24). And in *The Worlding of Jean Rhys*, Sue Thomas comments on Rhys's profound discomfort with the role her maternal ancestors played in Dominica's history of slavery and colonialism (33).

The novels of Jean Rhys continue to generate controversy. In her introduction to a special *Jean Rhys* issue of the *Journal of Caribbean Literatures*, guest editor Mary Lou Emery observes the "conflicting ideological positions" of many contributors on a wide range of subjects, including "Creole racism," canon formation, imperialism, patriarchy, "feminist Manicheanism," and divided subjectivity. These debates in Caribbean and postcolonial studies, claims Emery, demonstrate "the importance of Rhys's work to developments in these critical fields" (xii).

The character of Christophine, in *Wide Sargasso Sea*, is a lightning rod for such controversy. In her book *Territories of the Psyche*, Ann Simpson argues that despite Rhys's distrust of psychoanalysis, it "offers the most powerful theoretical paradigm to date for exploring the complexities of emotional life as these are expressed in literature as well as life" (12). Citing Melanie Klein, Simpson sees Christophine as "the giving mother of the good breast" in contrast to Antoinette's biological mother whose "dry and life-denying behavior" makes her the "bad breast" (115). In *Home, Maison, Casa*, Erica Johnson stresses the ideological force of "home" as a "psychological, geographical as well as social concept" in narratives of empire (13). The centrality of Christophine to Rhys's narrative is seen in her "acute sense of the importance of place" which "lays bare the machinations through which Rochester works to appropriate his wife's identity, as is evident in the juxtapositioning of her conversations with Antoinette and Rochester" (101). Writing in the special issue of *JCLs* about the importance of names and naming in *Wide Sargasso Sea*, Maria Cristina Fumagalli agrees "with Foucault that a proper name is the equivalent of a description," and therefore Christophine's name, with its horticultural and historical significance, facilitates her "counter-discourse" which is "deeply-rooted in Caribbean soil," to an extent transforming Christophine into "what the Romans called a *genius loci*, a protective spirit resident in a specific place" (129-130).

In contrast to these positive readings of Christophine's role in *Wide Sargasso Sea*, Victoria Burrows, in *Whiteness and Trauma*, finds evidence of "cultural appropriation" in "the installation of a central black voice in the novel to espouse the white Creole point of view with a strong sense of empathy" (31). Burrows does not deny Christophine's strength but questions its source: "It is left to Christophine to critique imperialist white masculinity, but not from the point of view of her own people. Her critique, a defense of Antonette, her much loved surrogate daughter, is from a white Creole perspective" (38). Burrows also takes issue with the fact that Christophine's "speech is always filtered through the consciousness of the white characters" (38).

Two other contributors to the special issue of *JCLs*, Elaine Savory and Joseph Clarke, weigh in with similar objections. Savory finds it "somewhat odd that Christophine, in *Wide Sargasso Sea*, has a problematically idealized character, just as Annette, the mother figure, is ideally beautiful and defenseless" ("Selective Memory" 21). Rejecting the notion that *Wide Sargasso Sea* is unequivocally anti-imperialist, Savory sees Christophine and Annette as "stock characters" from "a Gothic white Creole romance" (23).

In his critique of Jean Rhys's third novel, *Voyage in the Dark*, Joseph Clarke observes Rhys's "inability to offer to the Afro-Caribbean other the subjective presence that is demanded for white women" (4). Clarke argues that Rhys's treatment of Maillote Boyd is the novel's first example of "Caribbean Africanism." He sees this as "part of a general economy of Caribbean modernism which [he calls] 'Creole modernism'" (4-5): a willful blindness to the socio-economic concerns of black West Indians and "the inability to write Afro-Caribbeans into the social contract" (11). In this important essay, Clarke, like Brathwaite before him, is challenging Anglophone Caribbean discourse to move beyond hegemonic Eurocritical "wonderland paradigms" and meet the Afro-Caribbean artist/scholar in his yard. I am concerned, however, that Rhys criticism has become too politicized and polarized. While there is no denying that Rhys uses primitivist or Africanist tropes to reimagine the role of the white Creole in the Caribbean, her relationship with her black characters and with the legacy of slavery and colonialism is complicated. Anna's invocation of Maillotte Boyd will serve as an example.

Fairly early in *Voyage in the Dark*, Anna remembers a slave list she once saw at Constance Estate, which had belonged to her mother's family for generations. One name stands out in Anna's memory, that of a young slave woman the same age that Anna is now: "Maillotte Boyd, aged 18, mulatto, house servant" (53). After making love to Walter Jeffries, an affluent Englishman much older than Anna, she again thinks of the young slave woman: "*Maillotte Boyd, aged 18. Maillotte Boyd, aged 18. . . . But I like it like this. I don't want it any other way but this*" (56). Unlike Joseph Clarke, who views this as "the story of Anna's sexual liberation" (6), I see Anna's affair as sexual bondage. Anna equates her sexual and emotional ties to Walter with slavery, and she not only accepts her fate but revels in it. By means of reckless, self-destructive sexual abandonment with a man who exploits and eventually rejects her, Anna imaginatively changes places with Maillotte Boyd and fulfills a prophecy made years earlier by Anna's English stepmother: "The sins of the fathers Hester said are visited upon the children unto the third and fourth generation" (53). The pain and suffering that Anna feels after Walter discards her can be seen as punishment for the sins of her mother's family, the Costeruses. Anna's voyage into the underworld of cheap hotels and drunken encounters with strange men, as well as her near fatal abortion—which *was* fatal in Rhys's earlier, preferred ending (Rhys, *Letters* 236-7)—is Anna's self-sacrificial offering. Like the Carib Indians Anna read about as a child, she and her kind, descendants of the slave-owning planter class, "are now practically exterminated" (105).

Viewing Rhys's novels against the background of Caribbean colonial history helps to explain many attributes of the so-called "Rhys woman": her self-destructive behavior, apparent passivity, sexual debasement, and fatalism. Rhys absorbed some of the tenets of Roman Catholicism during her youth in Dominica (Savory 110), and her novels constitute a somewhat twisted tale of remorse and repentance for the white Creole's complicity in slavery and colonial domination. This is especially true of Rhys's last novel, *Wide Sargasso Sea*. Antoinette's nemesis, Daniel Cosway, a self-styled harbinger of retribution, claims to be one of the many illegitimate children of Antoinette's father, a man who was notorious for having sexual relations with his female slaves. Daniel can only hope that the "damn devil my father" is burning in hell for his sins (*WSS* 122). Not satisfied with the possibility of divine retribution, however, Daniel—who claims that his real name is Esau—proceeds to ensure that old Cosway's only surviving legitimate child, Antoinette, is made to suffer for the sins of her father. It is Daniel who convinces Antoinette's husband that he has been tricked into marrying an intemperate, promiscuous, unstable woman. Daniel also gives the husband the ammunition he needs to banish Christophine, leaving Antoinette alone and friendless. Even more directly than in *Voyage in the Dark*, the father's sins are visited upon his offspring, with Antoinette becoming the most clearly defined of Rhys's sacrificial victims.

Antoinette's complicity in her own tragic fate might seem inexplicably self-destructive unless it is viewed as her predestined part in a centuries-long historical drama. Her awareness of her destiny becomes apparent the second time she has her recurring dream of following a man who hates her through a dense forest: "I follow him, sick with fear but I make no effort to save myself; if anyone were to try to save me, I would refuse. This must happen" (*WSS* 59-60). Christophine and Sandi do try to save her, but she spurns their advice and assistance because *this must happen*. Antoinette is the product of historical forces that dwarf the needs and desires of any one individual. Her narrative opened with allusions to Genesis and the Garden of Eden, which immediately placed the historic events surrounding the novel—the Emancipation Act and the decline of the planter class—within a mythic framework. Antoinette's world was destined to fall because it was rotten at the core, and her fate, her role in this historic drama, is to pay with her life for the sins of her forefathers: "This must happen" (60).

Antoinette is a *willing* victim, a sacrificial offering, not a scapegoat. Unlike Bertha Rochester in *Jane Eyre*, who appears wholly at the mercy of her husband until her final desperate act, Antoinette has foreseen her destiny in dreams since childhood and has manipulated events to achieve her goal: e.g., agreeing to a loveless marriage; allowing the seductive Amelie to live in close proximity to the newlyweds; poisoning her husband with the "love" potion that Christophine had warned her was "bad trouble" when used by white people. Her husband may control her body and material possessions, but Antoinette has sabotaged his soul and robbed him of joy. He reflects on what he has lost at the end of the novel: "So I shall never understand why, suddenly, bewilderingly, I was certain that everything I had imagined to be truth was false. False. Only the magic and the dream are true—all the rest's a lie. Let it go. Here is the secret. Here. (*But it is lost, that secret, and those who know it cannot tell it.*)" (167-8). By assigning him a key role in her personal drama of remorse and self-sacrifice on the altar of Caribbean history, Antoinette has undermined her husband's faith in patriarchy, in Christianity, and in the innate superiority of the upper-class Englishman. His revenge will be swift and dire, but Antoinette's victory is signified by the fact that in Rhys's novel, Rochester remains nameless and must be referred to in the possessive case as Antoinette's husband: "I have not bought her, she has bought me, or so she thinks" (*WSS* 70). Of course, there are no real winners in this gender and culture based conflict, but Antoinette falls to her death with her anger and pride still intact because, as Rhys explained to Francis Wyndham, Antoinette "hates last" (*Letters* 263).

In a review of the movie based on *Wide Sargasso Sea*, Jamaican-born writer Michelle Cliff comments: "I emerged from a world that deserved to die, one that had changed little from the time of *Wide Sargasso Sea* to the time of my girlhood" (78). By observing that the world she grew up in had changed little from post-Emancipation Jamaica as imagined by Jean Rhys, Cliff undermines the validity of the term "post-colonial." Kamau Brathwaite is more direct:

> What I continue to maintain is that too many nonCalibans* & now 'post-colonialist' critics are trying to shift Rhys'figment & 'guilt' onto Tia & 'me' & I RESENT this. I also resent the notion of 'post-colonial' applied so easily to our **neo-colonial** condition, its false premises of FIGMENT strategically (re)designed to continue the OLD STORY. (74)

Most of the critical studies discussed in this essay indicate that Jean Rhys criticism is moving away from the race-neutral, ahistoric approaches that Brathwaite views as a way of masking or denying or reassigning white guilt. The fascination that Jean Rhys holds for many white readers reflects a recognition of our own complicity in the historical drama that continues to foster injustice toward people of color throughout the world. The novels of Jean Rhys remind us that "what's past is prologue; what to come, in mine and your discharge" (*The Tempest*, II, i, 261-2).

Works Cited

Brathwaite, Kamau. "A Post-Cautionary Tale of the Helen of Our Wars." *Wasafiri* 22 (Autumn 1995): 69-81.

Burrows, Victoria. *Whiteness and Trauma: The Mother-Daughter Knot in the Fiction of Jean Rhys, Jamaica Kincaid and Toni Morrison.* Hampshire and New York: Palgrave Macmillan, 2004.

Clarke, Joseph. "Caribbean Modernism and the Postcolonial Social Contract in *Voyage in the Dark.*" *Jean Rhys.* Ed. Mary Lou Emery. Spec. issue of *Journal of Caribbean Literatures* 3.3 (2003): 1-16.

Cliff, Michelle. "Adrift in Female Terrain." *Ms.* July/August 1993: 76-78.

Emery, Mary Lou, guest ed. *Jean Rhys.* Special issue of *Journal of Caribbean Literatures* 3.3. (2003).

———. "Misfit: Jean Rhys and the Visual Cultures of Colonial Modernism." *Jean Rhys.* Ed. Mary Lou Emery. Spec. issue of *Journal of Caribbean Literatures* 3.3 (2003): xi-xxii.

Fumagalli, Maria Cristina. "Names Matter." *Jean Rhys.* Ed. Mary Lou Emery. Spec. issue of *Journal of Caribbean Literatures* 3.3 (2003):123-132.

Gregg, Veronica Marie. *Jean Rhys's Historical Imagination: Reading and Writing the Creole.* Chapel Hill: University of North Carolina Press, 1995.

Hulme, Peter. "The Place of *Wide Sargasso Sea.*" *Wasafiri* 20 (Autumn, 1994): 5-11.

Johnson, Erica L. *Home, Maison, Casa: The Politics of Location in Works by Jean Rhys, Marguerite Duras, and Erminia Dell'Oro.* Madison and Teaneck: Fairleigh Dickinson University Press, 2003.

Rhys, Jean. *The Letters of Jean Rhys.* Ed. Francis Wyndham and Diana Melly. Elizabeth Sifton Books. New York: Viking, 1984.

———. *Voyage in the Dark.* 1934. New York: Norton, 1982.

———. *Wide Sargasso Sea.* 1966. New York: Norton, 1982.

Savory, Elaine. *Jean Rhys.* Cambridge, UK: Cambridge University Press, 1998.

———. "Selective Memory: White Creole Nostalgia, Jean Rhys and *Side by Side.*" *Jean Rhys.* Ed. Mary Lou Emery. Spec. issue of *Journal of Caribbean Literatures* 3.3 (2003): 17-36.

Simpson, Anne B. *Territories of the Psyche: The Fiction of Jean Rhys.* Hampshire and New York: Palgrave Macmillan, 2005.

Thomas, Sue. *The Worlding of Jean Rhys.* Contributions to the Study of World Literature 96. Westport, CT: Greenwood, 1999.

About the Author

Lucy Wilson is a Professor of English at Loyola Marymount University in Los Angeles. She is currently working on a study of illness as metaphor in modern literature.